The Chord Scale Guide

Discover exciting new chords with linear harmonization

by Greg Cooper

Music Notation/Tab - Dore Rabinoff
Cover Art - Kristi Jorgensen
Cover Layout - Shawn Brown
Inside Ilustrations - James Koukos
Editor - Dore Rabinoff
Production - Nirvana Alonso

ISBN 1-57424-141-9
SAN 683-8022

Thanks...

Ron Veil, for being a great friend and master vintage amp restorer (unclespot.com)

Ron Middlebrook, my friend and publisher at Centerstream Publications

Jim Day for his friendship and recording services

Brad Wendkos and all at True Fire (truefire.com)

My Pop, James for his great "flash figures"
My Mother, Bette for her love and belief

Dedicated to Dore
For her love, patience, effort and understanding

In rememberance
Talmage "Tal" Farlow
(1924-1998)

Contents

Foreword...

After 25 years of teaching guitar, it still amazes me when new students excitedly bring me a chord book they've purchased from the local music store. Generally they're as thick as bibles and entice the unsuspecting six-string optimist with titles such as **"5,025,178 CHORDS!" or "EVERY CHORD KNOWN TO MAN! (and a couple he may have forgotten)".** You know the books I'm talking about. They were around in my day and they are still with us today.

I have yet to meet the student who has really retained most of the material represented within those types of books. The reasons being (1) they are learning shapes and patterns, and (2) the same shapes and patterns are moving up the neck and represented as "new" chords. This is done for filler and to fatten up the book.

In other words, the student hasn't any understanding as to individual harmony within the chord.

"THE CHORD SCALE GUIDE" will open up new voicings for chords and heighten awarness of linear harmonization. This will be beneficial to the jazz ensemble player as well as the rock guitarist and songwriters looking to create new and unique original music. PLUS, the student will understand the harmony behind the chord and not have to rely on "shapes and patterns"

Don't get me wrong, those books with 5,000 chords in them are good reference books, but do you walk around with a dictionary when having a conversation with your best friend? Doubtful...

Enjoy this book and use it to your best advantage.

Keep on Pluckin'
GC

What is a chord scale?

C = Root	
D = 2nd	
E = 3rd	
F = 4th	
G = 5th	
A = 6th	
B = 7th	

Well, let's take a single note scale in the key of **C Major** and play it on one string only. Our root **(C)** is on the **A** string and moves up the neck diatonically.

Example 1

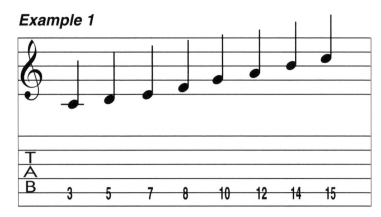

Let's harmonize our root wth a **Major 3rd (E)** and move that diatonically up the **D** string in the key of **C**.

Example 2

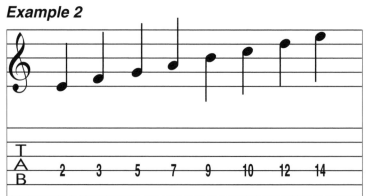

So, now we have, believe it or not, a chord scale! Remember, a chord is two or more notes. Two notes are called a **DIAD**.

Example 3

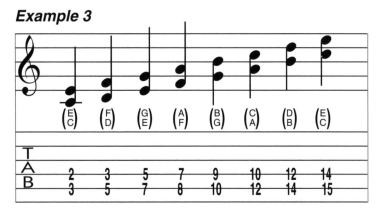

Let's harmonize the root **(C)** and the 3rd **(E)** together with a 5th **(G)** and move that up the neck in a linear fashion, forming a three note chord called a **TRIAD**.

Example 4

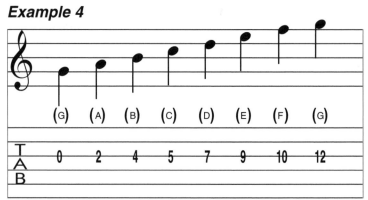

Combine all three harmonies, Root (C), 3rd (E), 5th (G), and you have....

...a chord scale

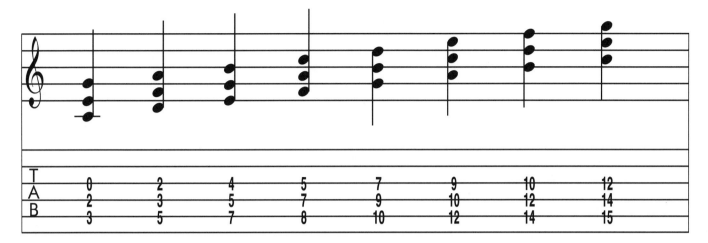

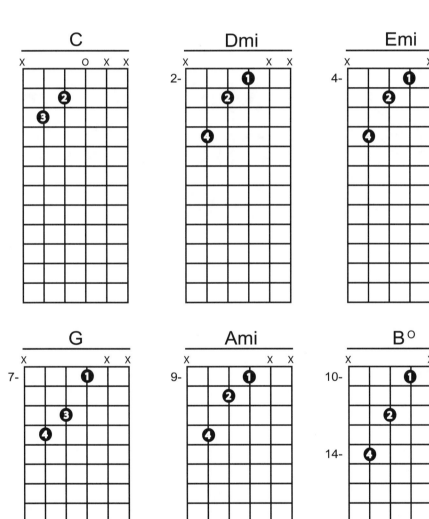

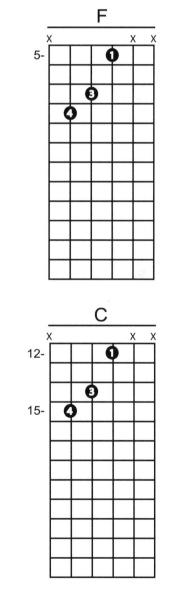

Major Chord Scales

| Major Triads |
| Major 6 |
| Major 6/9 |
| Major 7 |
| Major 9 |

Triad

Voicing - 5, Root, 3
Key - C

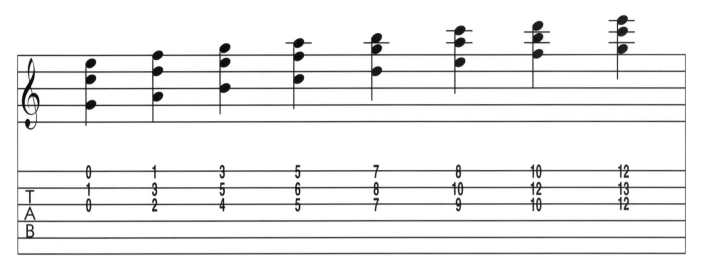

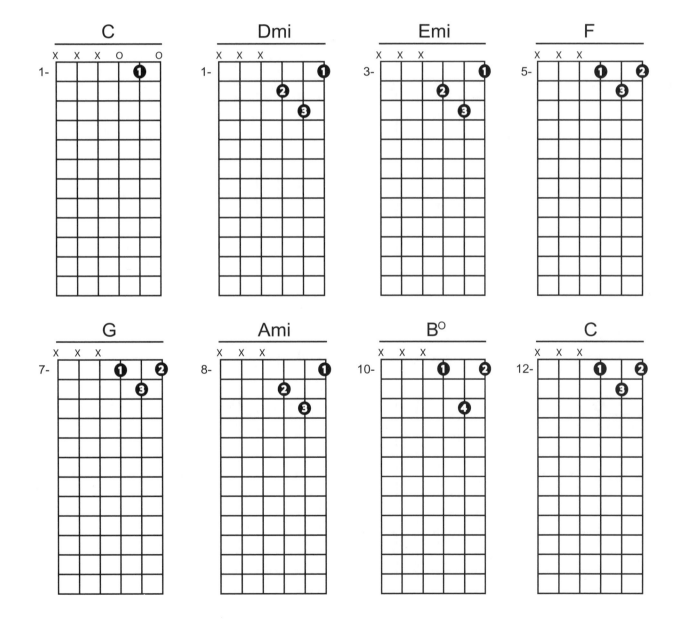

Triad
Voicing - 3, Root, 5
Key - C

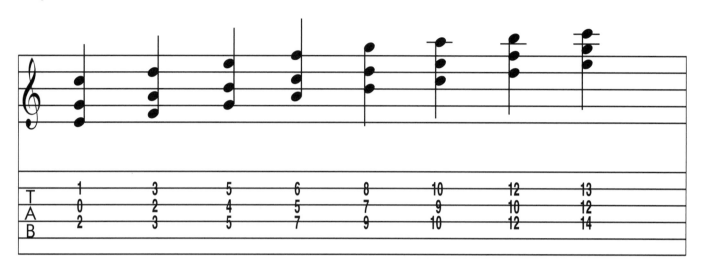

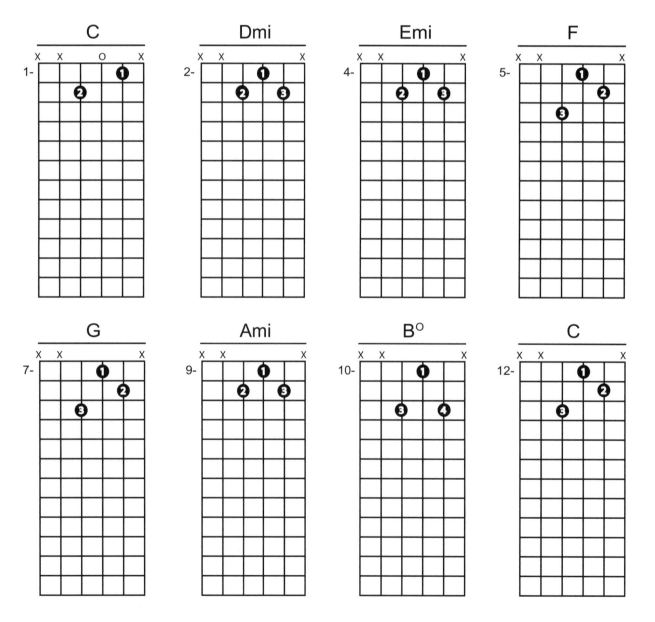

Triad

Voicing - Root, 5, 3
Key - C

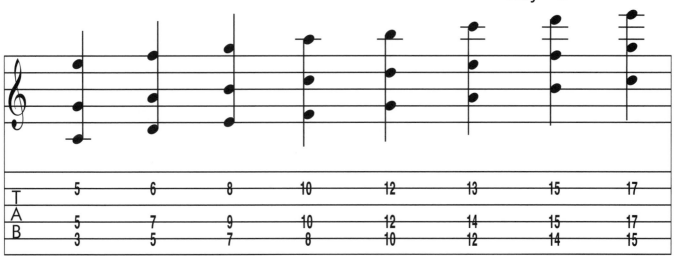

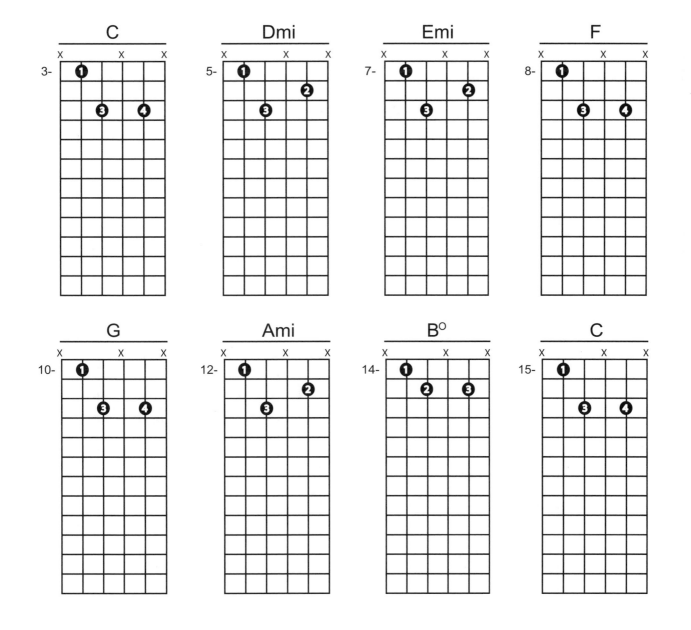

Triad

Voicing - 5, Root, 3
Key - C

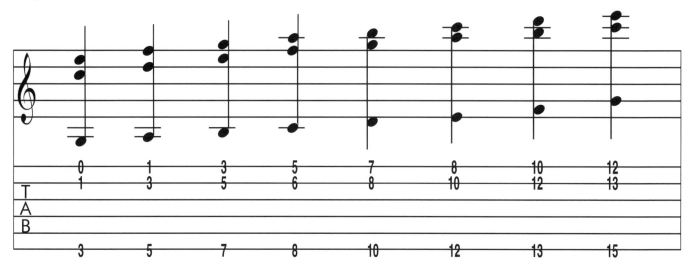

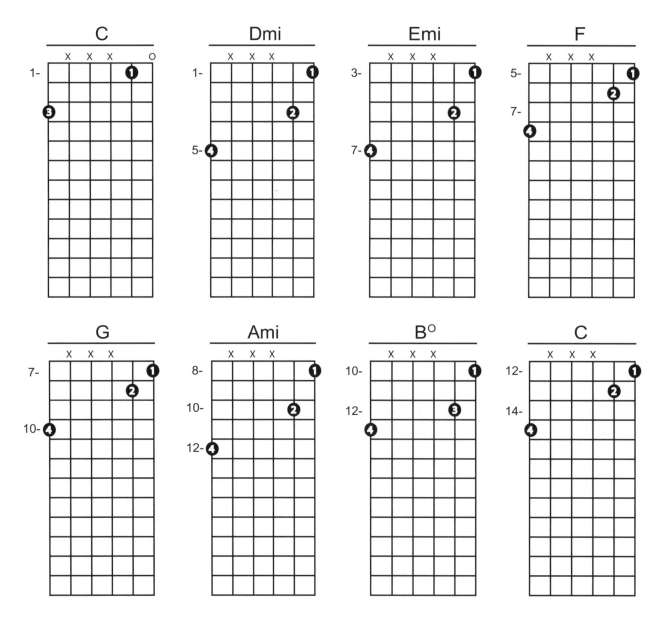

Triad
Voicing - 5, Root, 3
Key - C

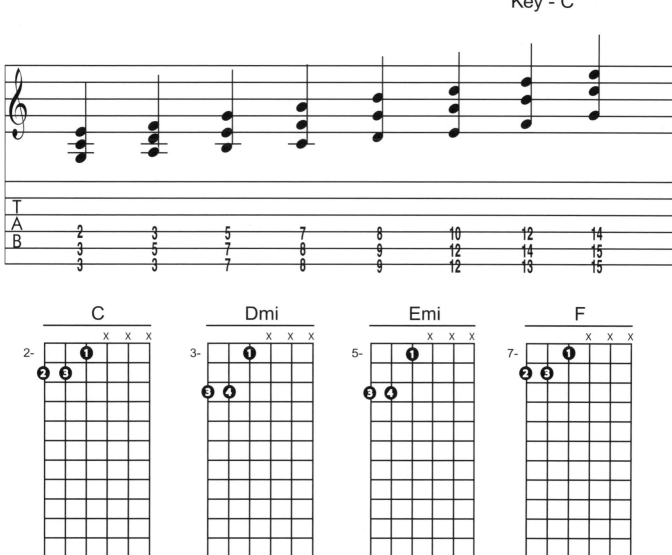

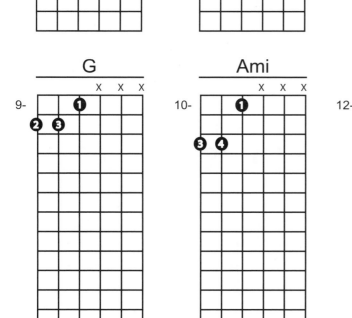

C   Dmi   Emi   F

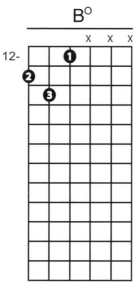 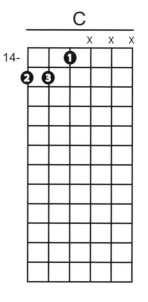

G   Ami   Bᵒ   C

Major 6
Voicing - Root, 5, 6, 3
Key - G

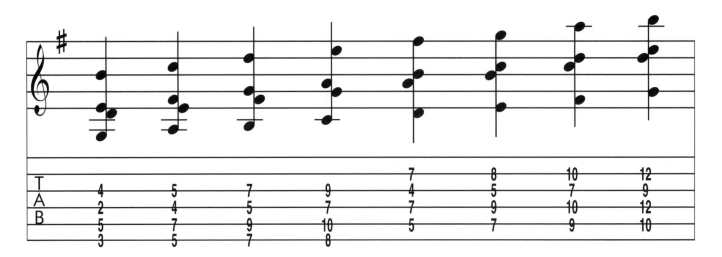

				7	8	10	12
4	5	7	9	4	5	7	9
2	4	5	7	7	9	10	12
5	7	9	10	5	7	9	10
3	5	7	8				

G6
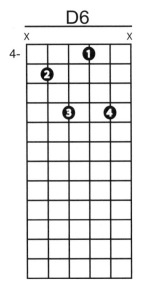

Ami6
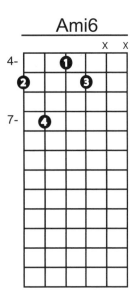

*Bmi♯5
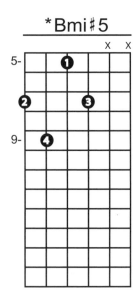

C6
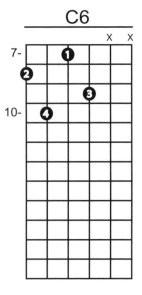

D6
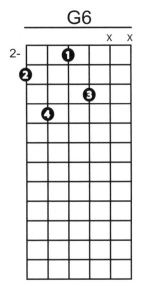

*Emi♯5
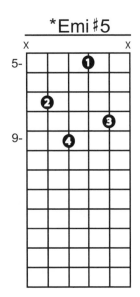

*F♯°♯5
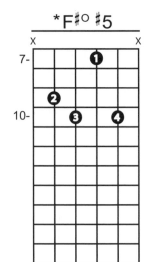

G6
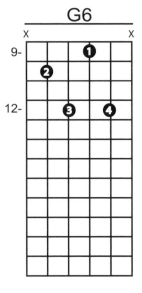

*Bmi♯5 = G MAJ7
Emi♯5 = C MAJ7
F♯°♯5 = D7

14

Major 6

Voicing - Root, 5, 6, 3

Key - F

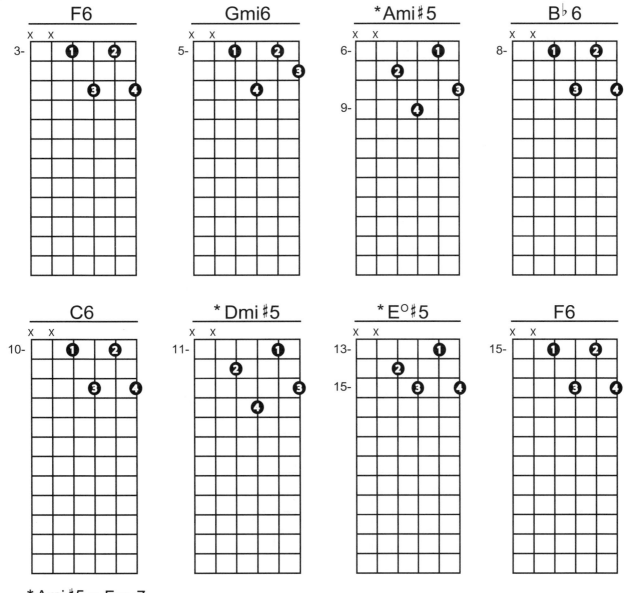

F6	Gmi6	*Ami#5	B♭6

C6	*Dmi#5	*E°#5	F6

*Ami#5 = F MAJ7

Dmi#5 = B♭ MAJ7

E°#5 = C7

15

Major 6

Voicing - 3, 6, Root, 5

Key - C

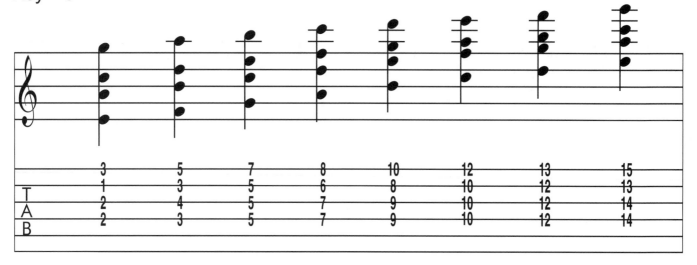

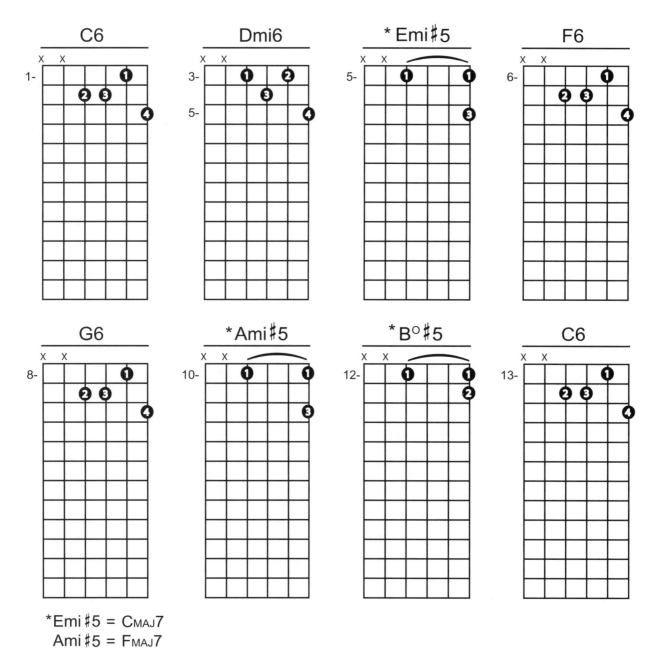

*Emi♯5 = C MAJ7

Ami♯5 = F MAJ7

B°♯5 = G7

16

Major 6/9

Voicing - R, 3, 6, 9
Key - C

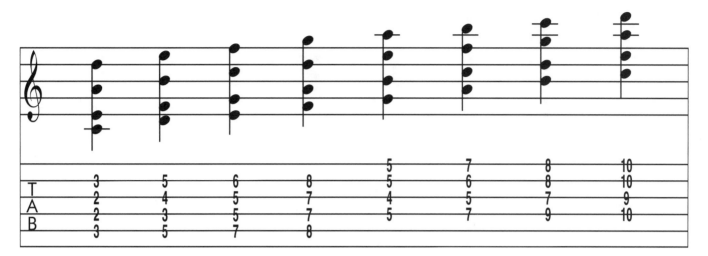

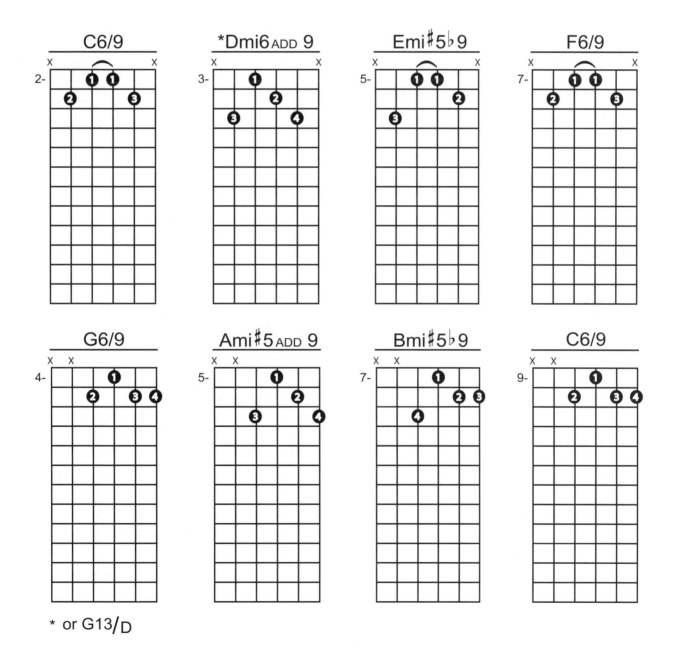

C6/9   *Dmi6 ADD 9   Emi♯5♭9   F6/9

G6/9   Ami♯5 ADD 9   Bmi♯5♭9   C6/9

* or G13/D

Major 7
Voicing - Root, 3, 5, 7
Key - C

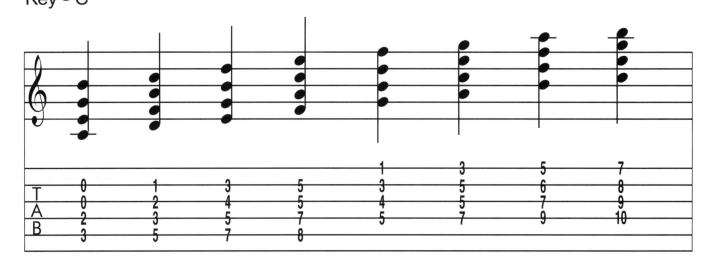

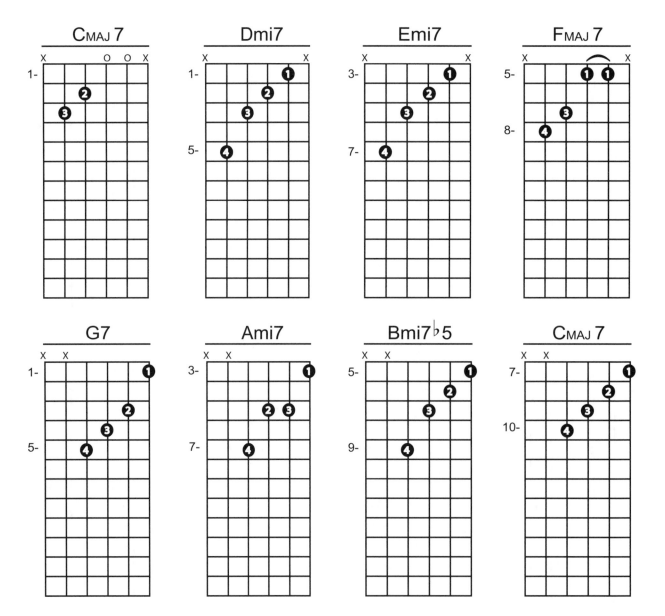

Major 7

Voicing - Root, 5, 7, 3
Key - C

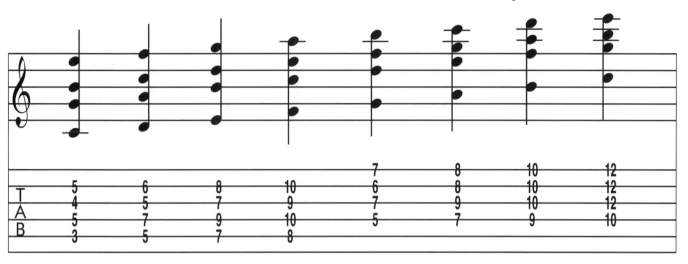

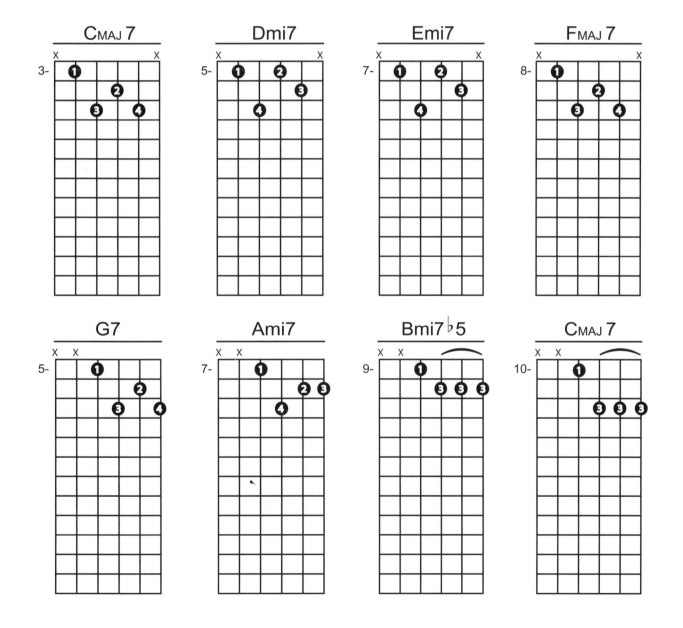

19

Major 7
Voicing - Root, 7, 3, 5
Key - C

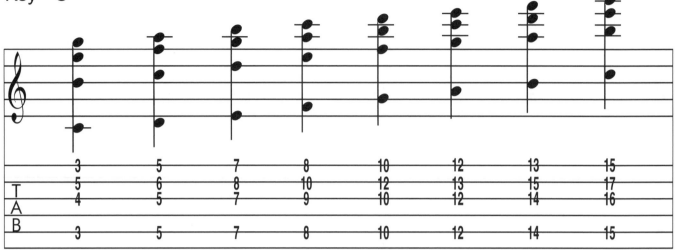

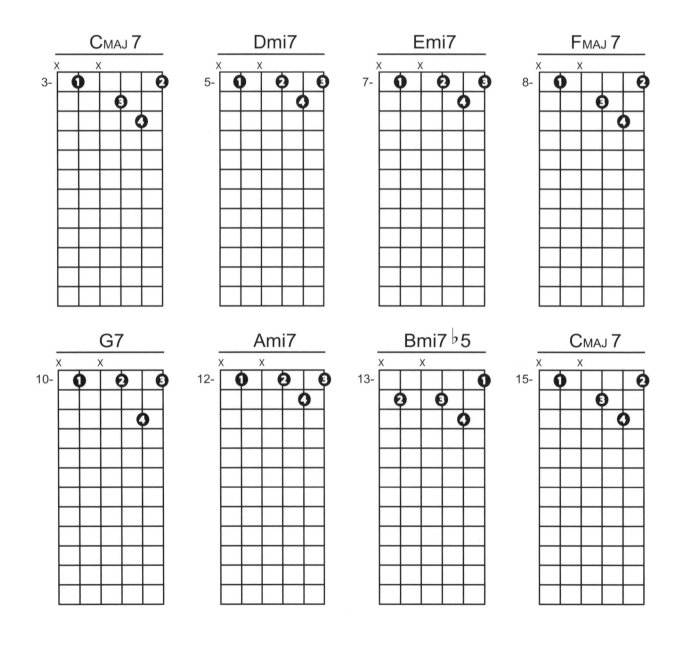

Major 7
Voicing - 3, 7, Root, 5
Key - F

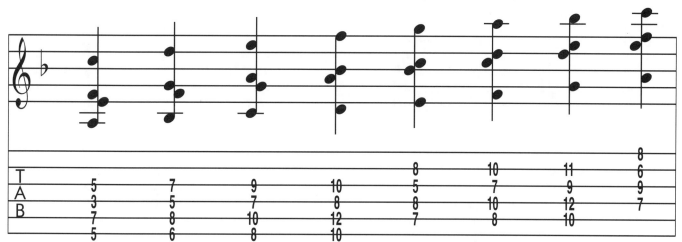

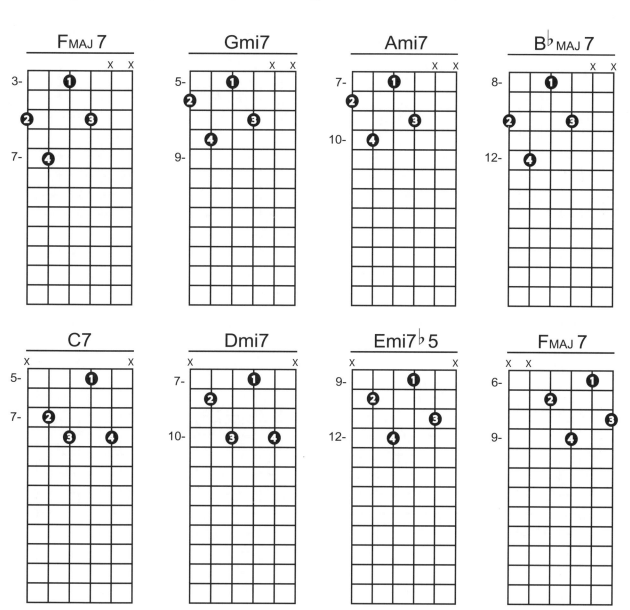

Major 7
Voicing - 5, Root, 3, 7
Key - C

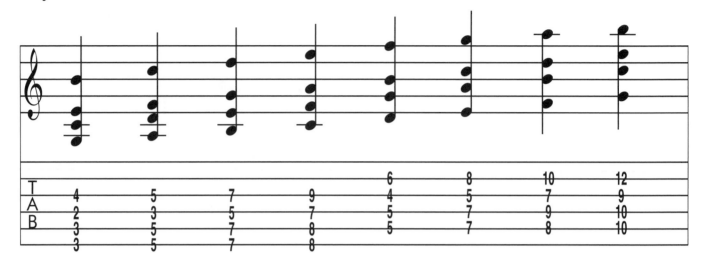

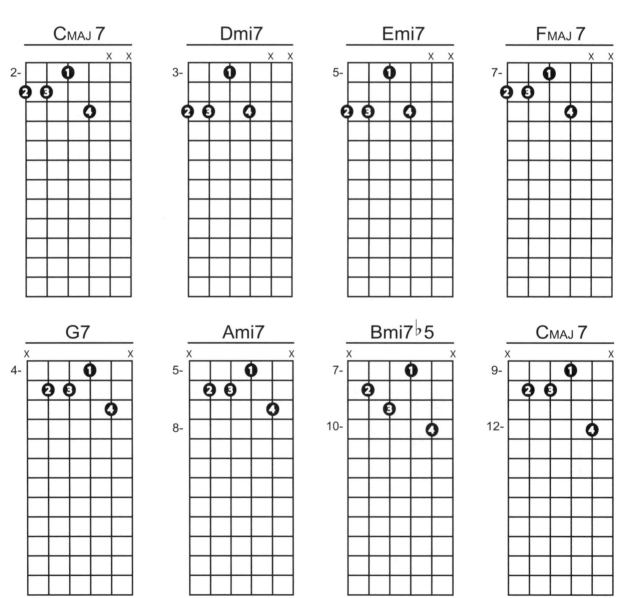

Major 7

Voicing - 3, 7, Root, 5
Key - C

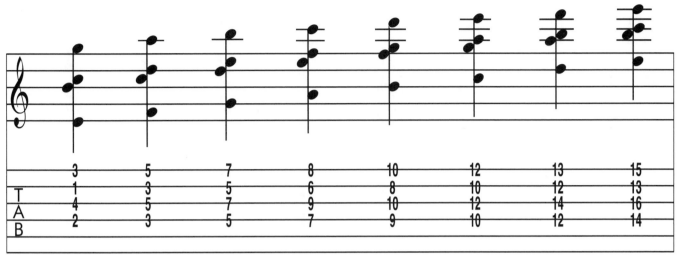

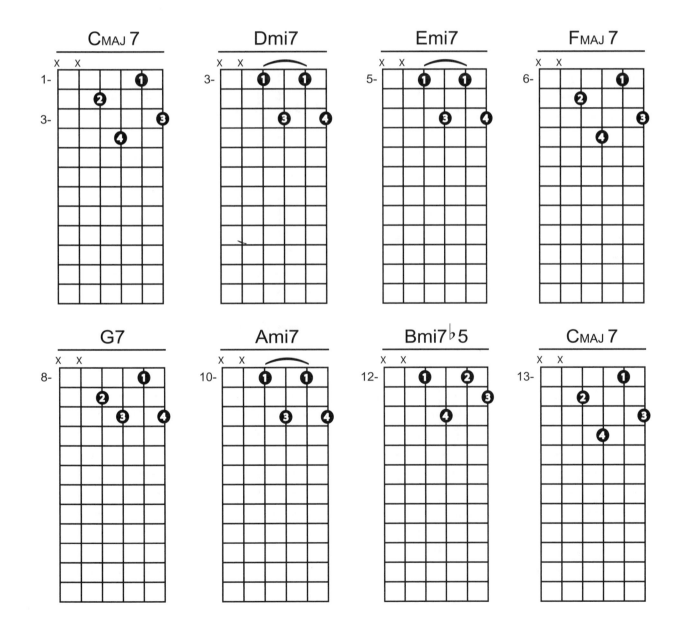

Major 7

Voicing - 5, Root, 3, 7
Key - C

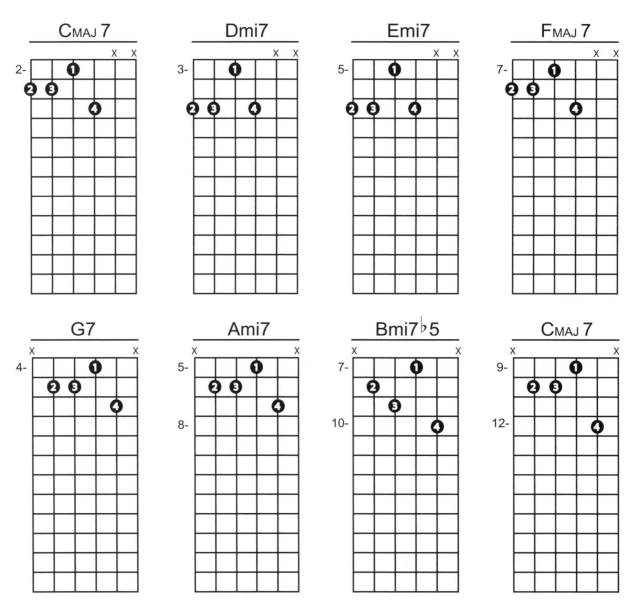

Major 9
Voicing - Root, 3, 7, 9
Key - C

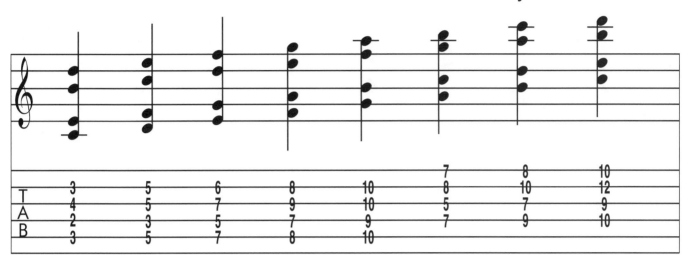

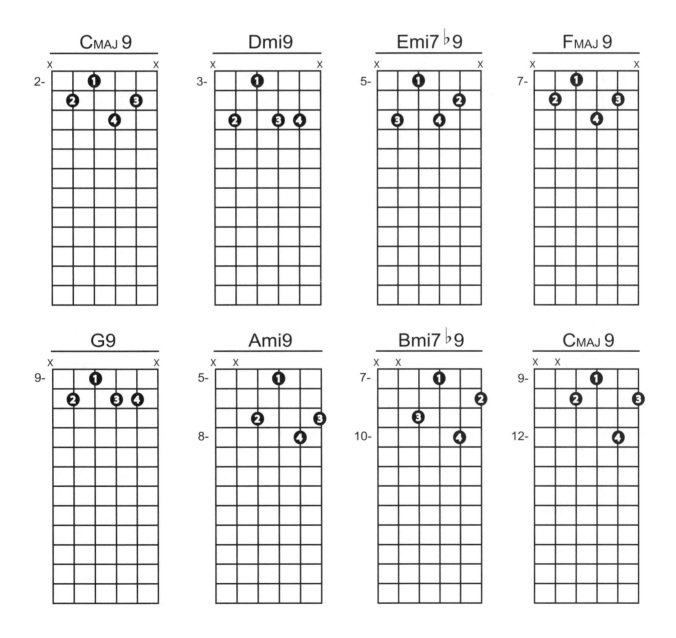

Major 9
Voicing - 7, 3, 5, 9
Key - F

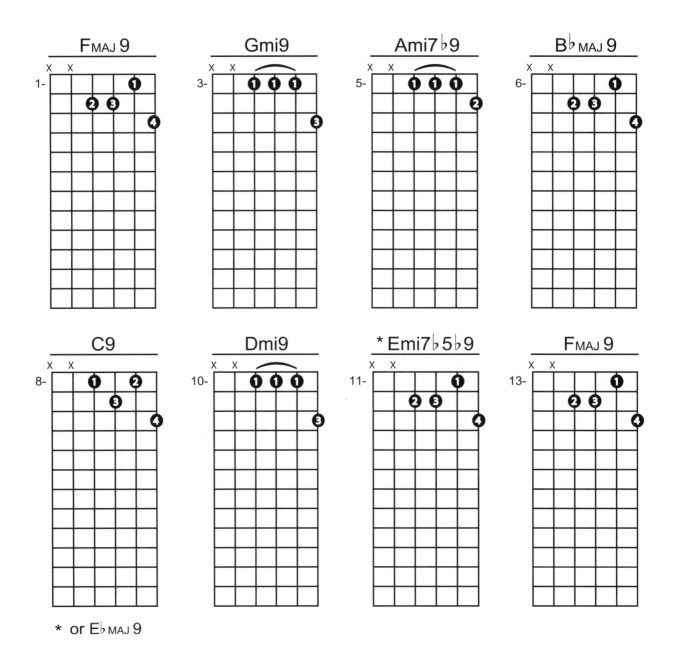

FMAJ 9 Gmi9 Ami7♭9 B♭MAJ 9

C9 Dmi9 *Emi7♭5♭9 FMAJ 9

* or E♭MAJ 9

26

Major 9

* Voicing - 7, 3, 5, 9
Key - C

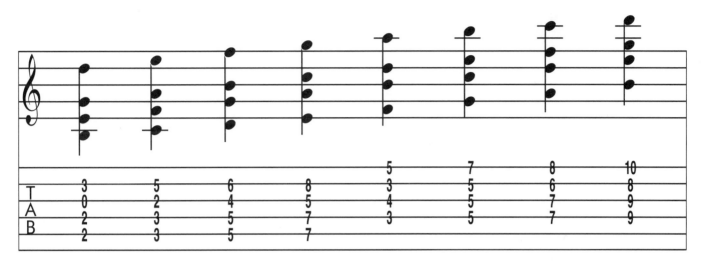

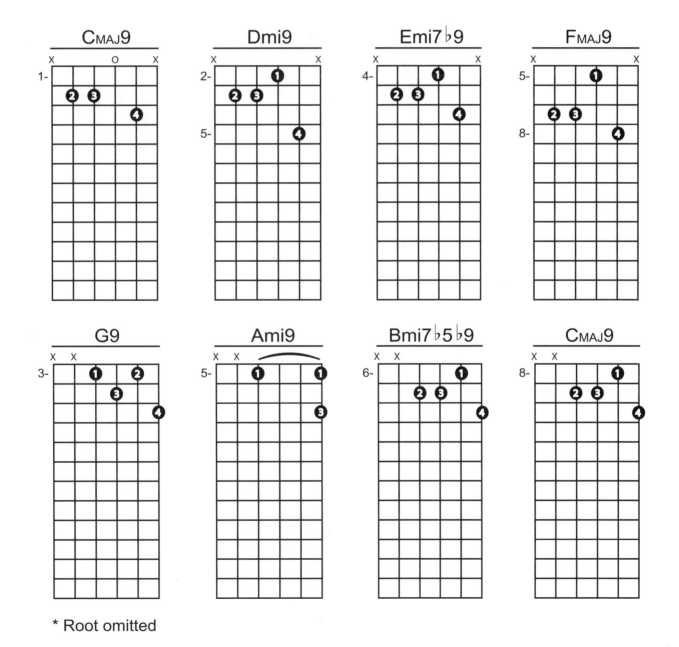

* Root omitted

27

Minor Chord Scales

Minor Triads
Minor 6
Minor 7
Minor 9

Pentatonic, Natural, Harmonic, Melodic

Minor Pentatonic Triad
Voicing - Root, ♭3, 5
Key - A Minor

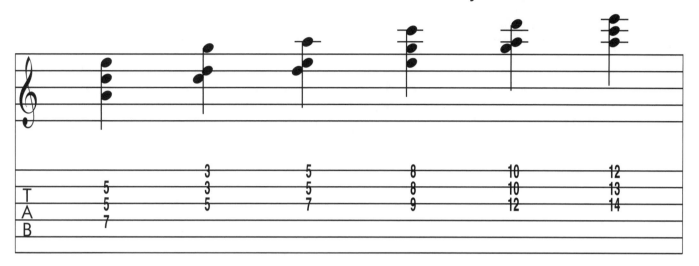

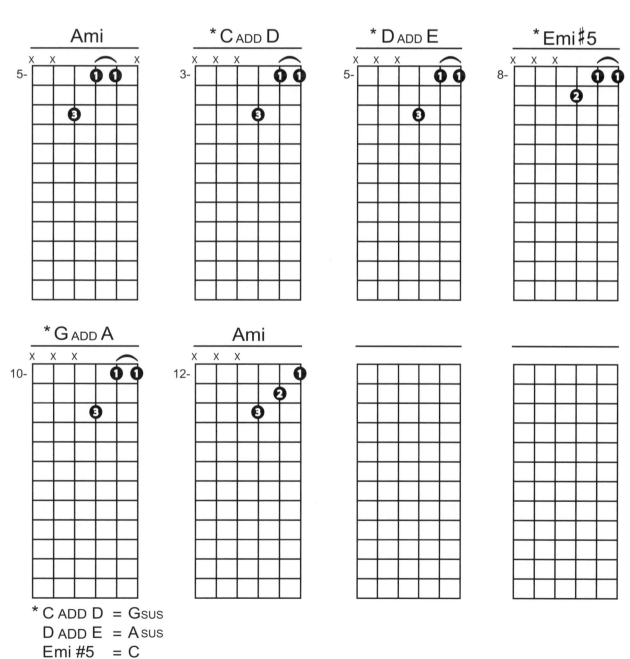

* C ADD D = Gsus
   D ADD E = Asus
   Emi #5   = C
   G ADD A = Dsus

Minor Pentatonic Triad
Voicing - Root, ♭3, 5
Key - A Minor

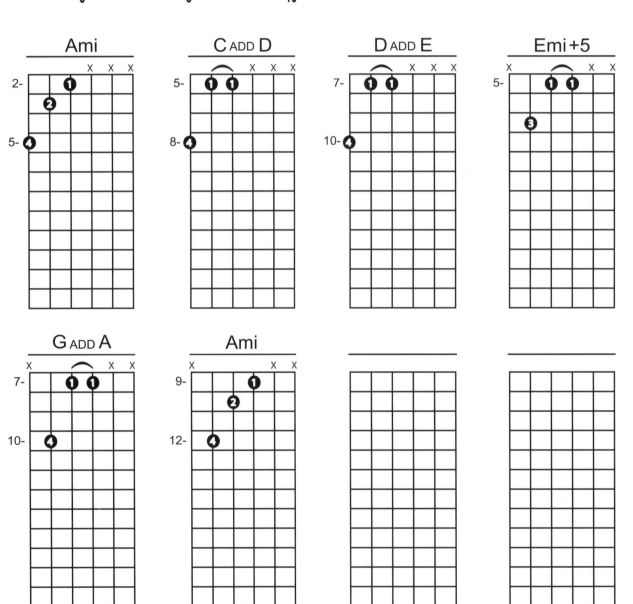

Minor Pentatonic Triad

Voicing - 5, Root, $\flat$3, $\flat$7

Key - A Minor

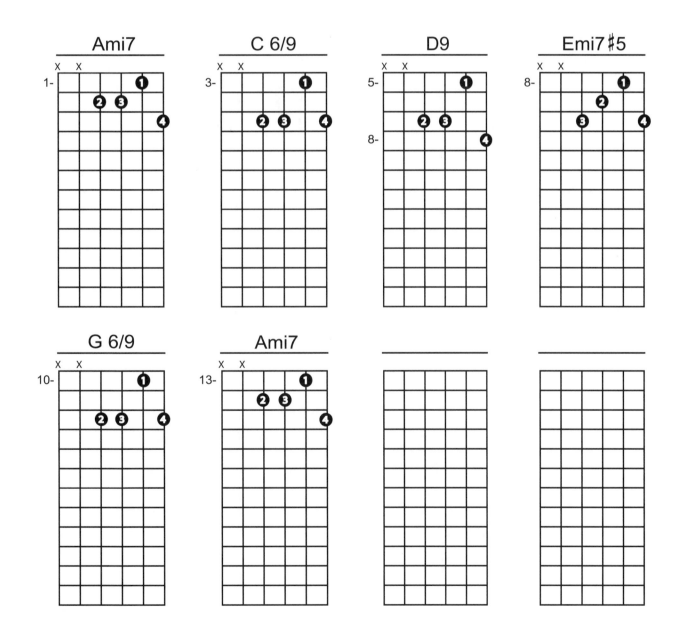

Natural Minor Triad
Voicing - Root, ♭3, 5
Key - D Minor

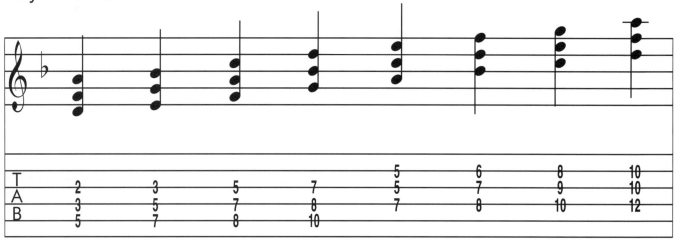

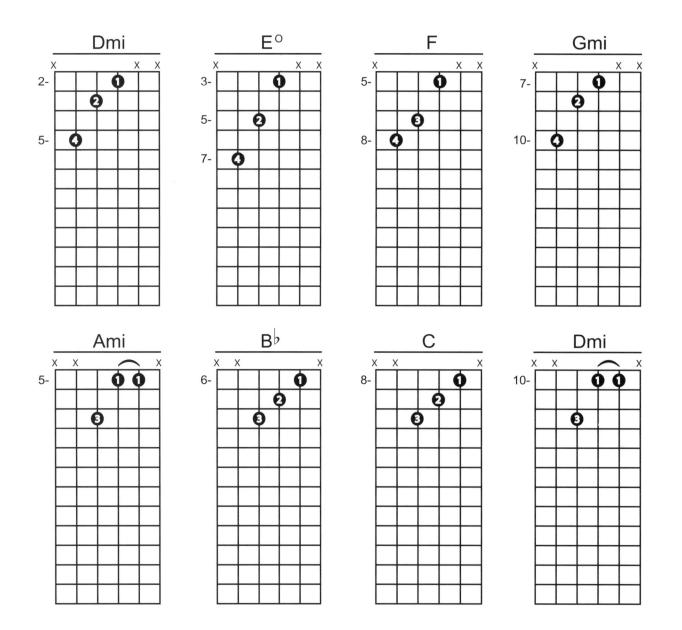

Natural Minor Triad
Voicing - Root, 5,♭3
Key - D Minor

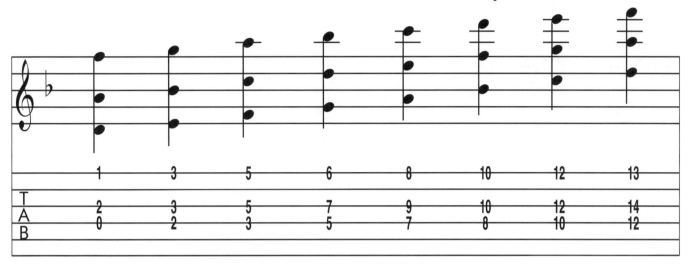

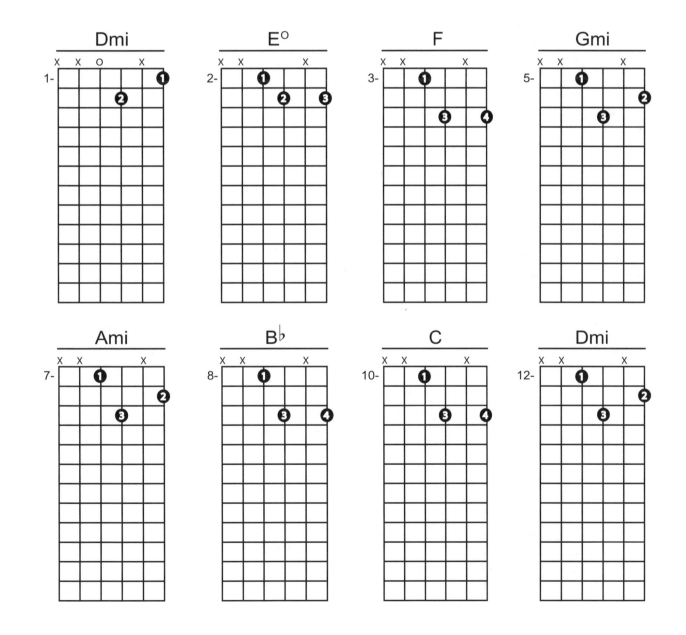

Natural Minor Triad
Voicing - Root, 5, ♭3
Key - A Minor

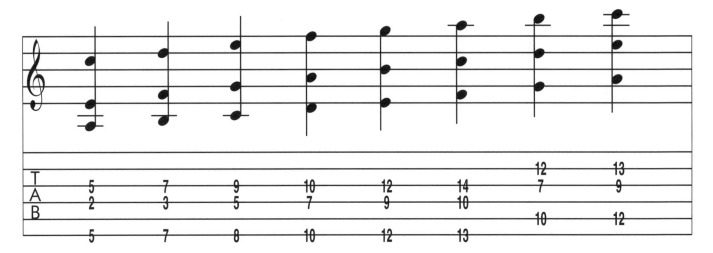

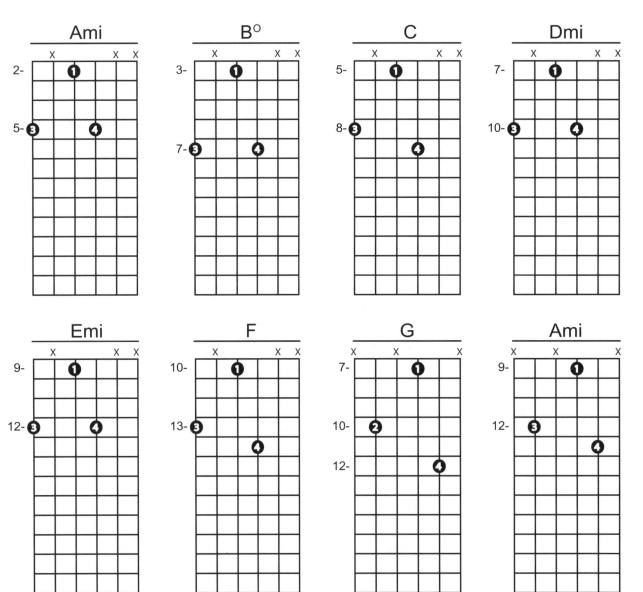

Natural Minor Triad
Voicing - Root, 5, ♭3
Key - E Minor

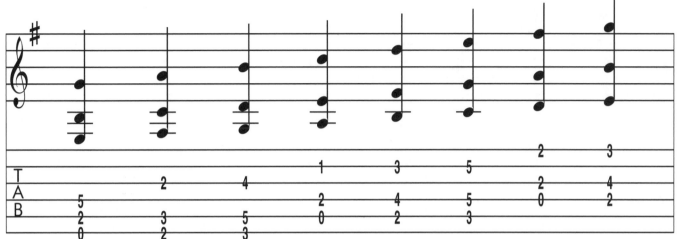

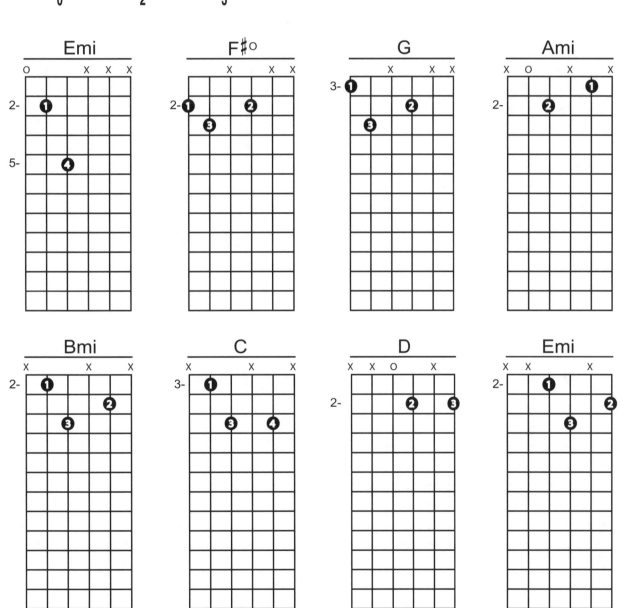

Natural Minor Triad

Voicing - ♭3, Root, 5

Key - D Minor

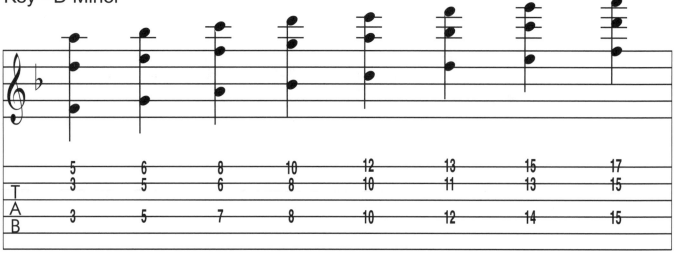

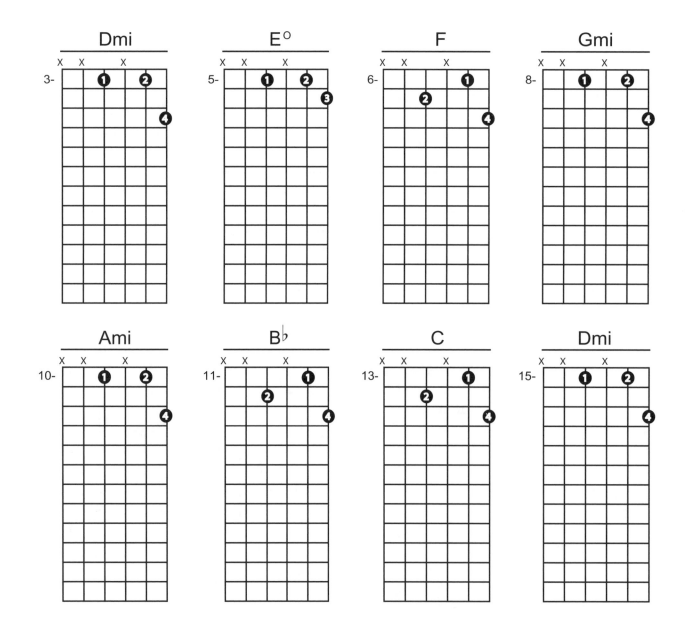

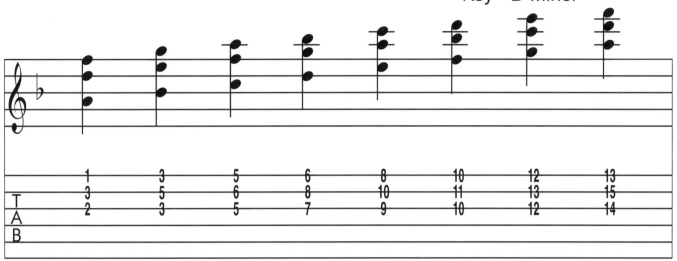

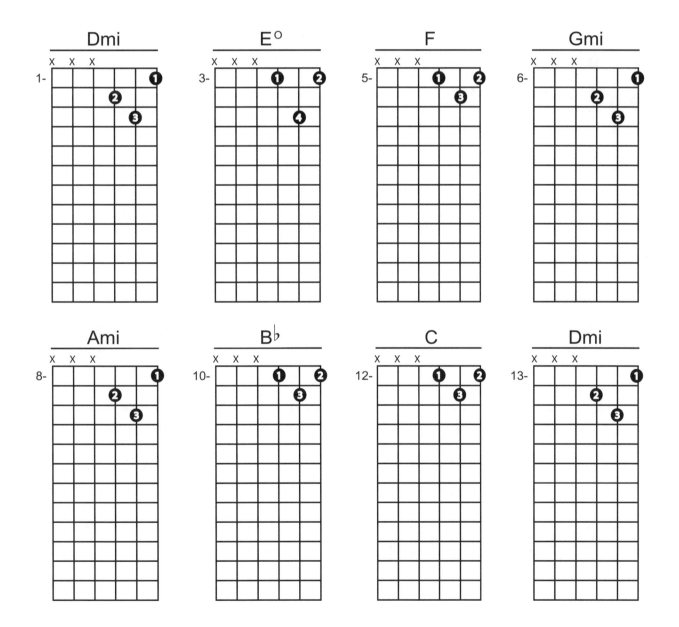

Natural Minor Triad
Voicing - 5, Root, ♭3
Key - D Minor

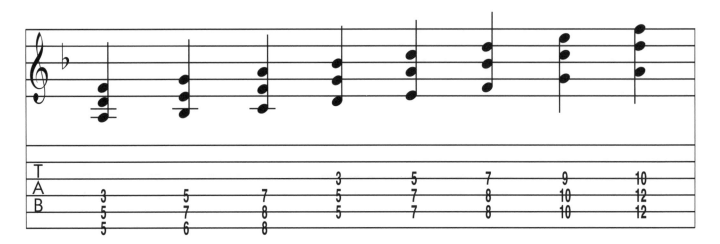

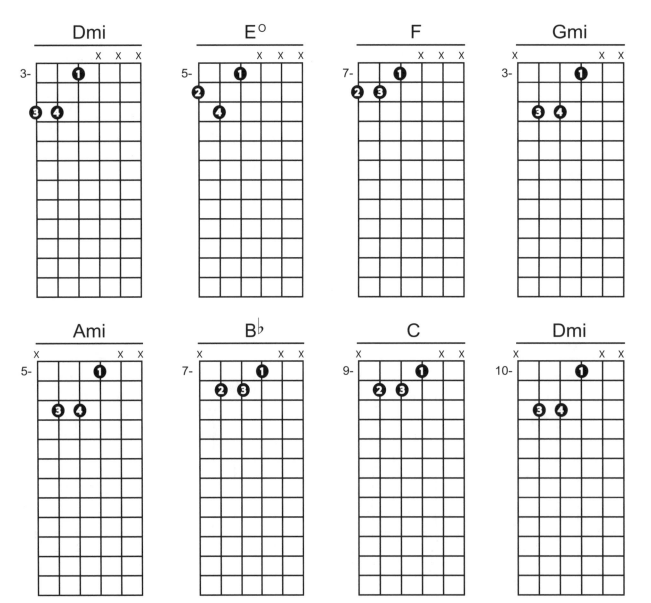

Natural Minor 7
Voicing - Root ♭7, ♭3, 5
Key - A Minor

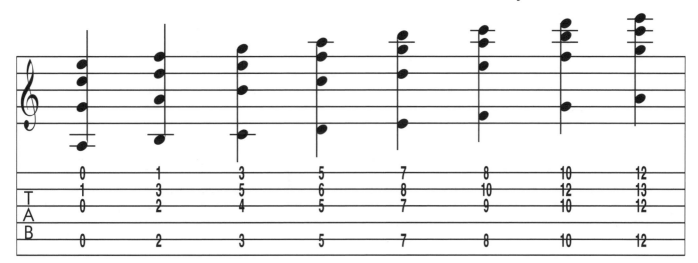

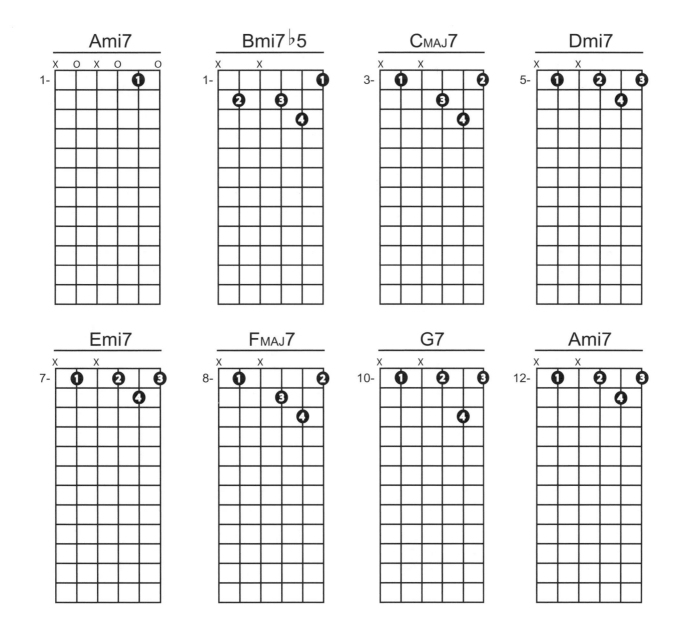

Natural Minor 7

Voicing - 5, Root, ♭3, ♭7

Key - A Minor

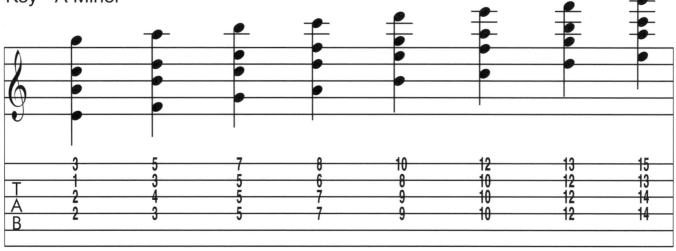

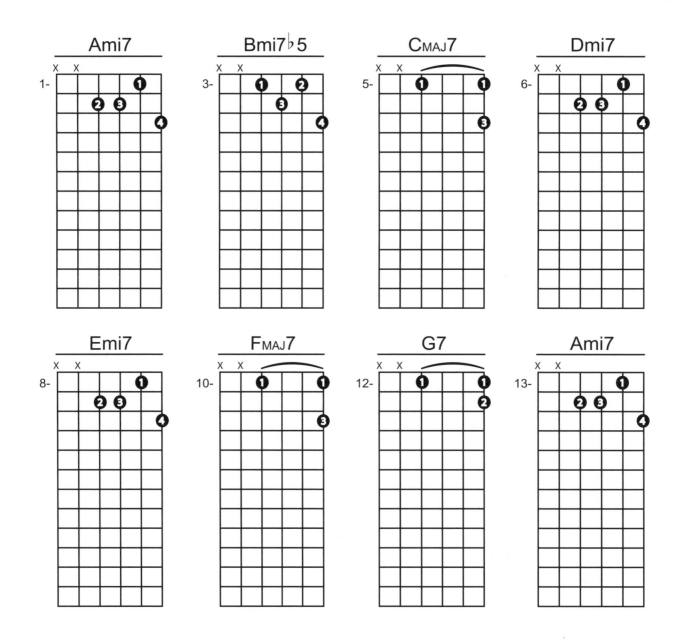

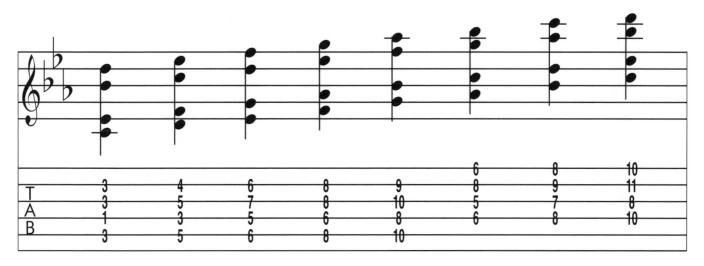

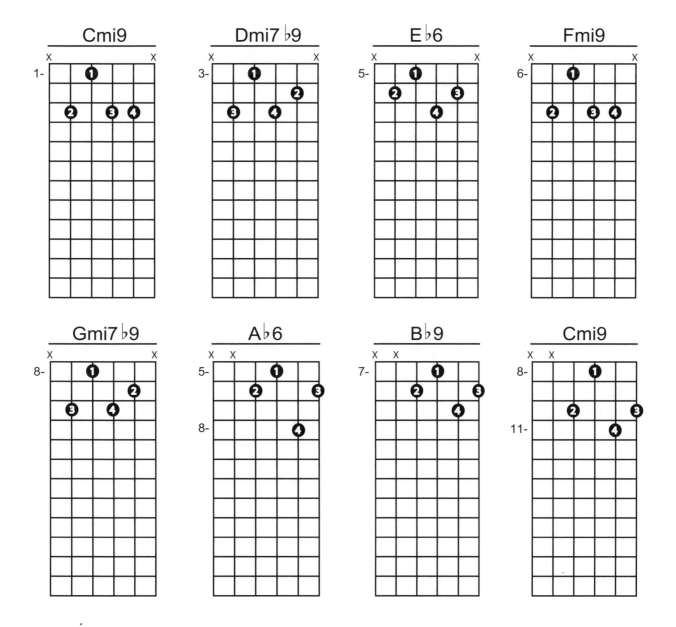

Natural Minor 9
Voicing - 5, 9, ♭3, ♭7
Key - E Minor

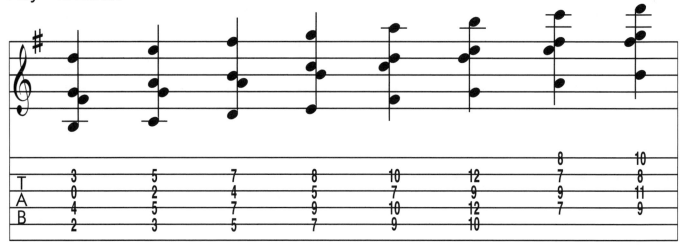

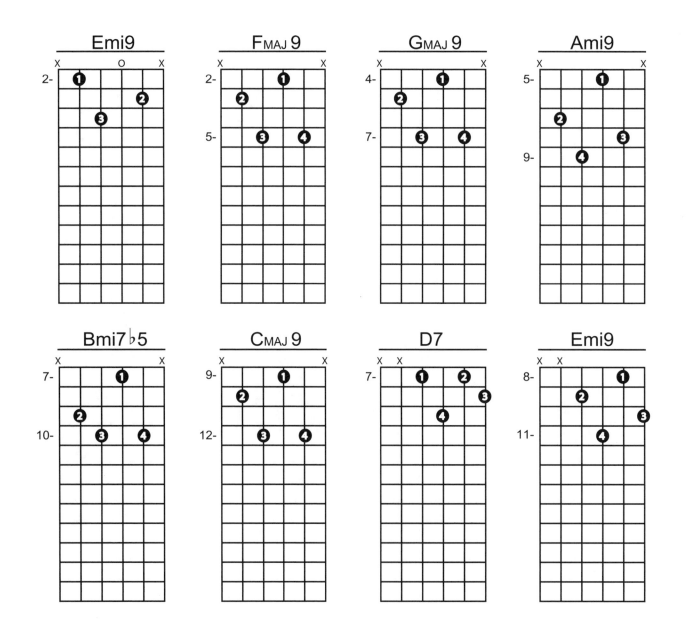

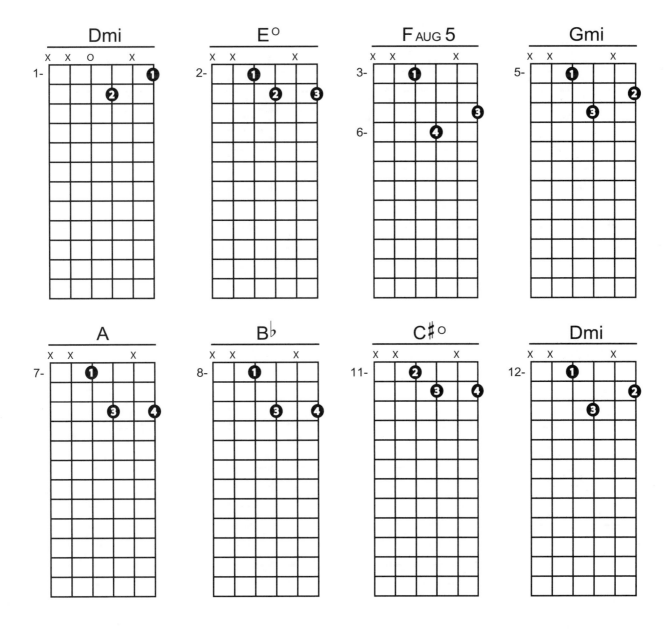

Harmonic Minor Triad
Voicing - Root, 5, ♭3
Key - A Minor

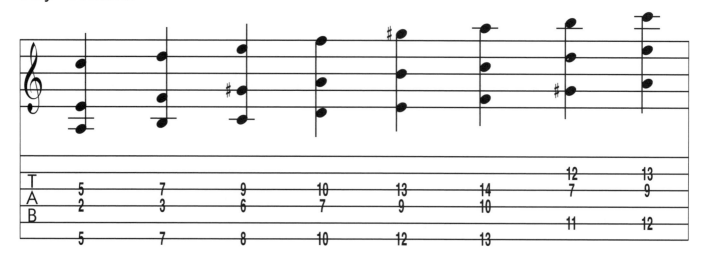

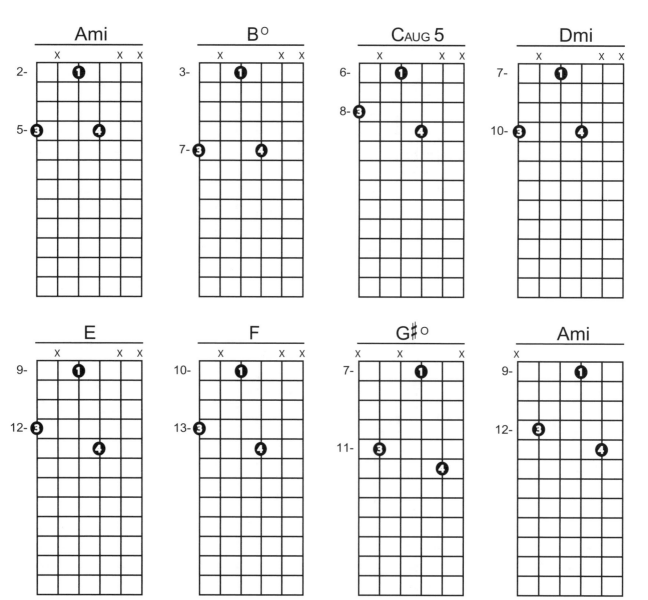

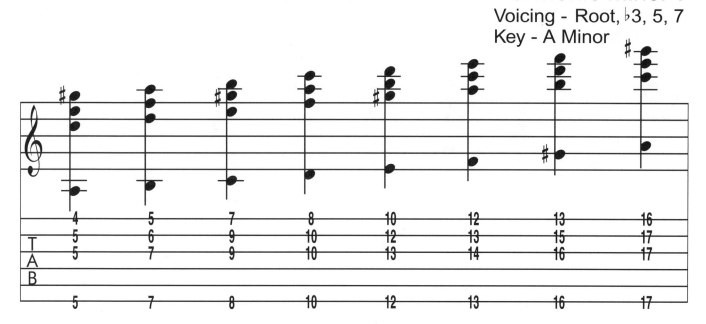

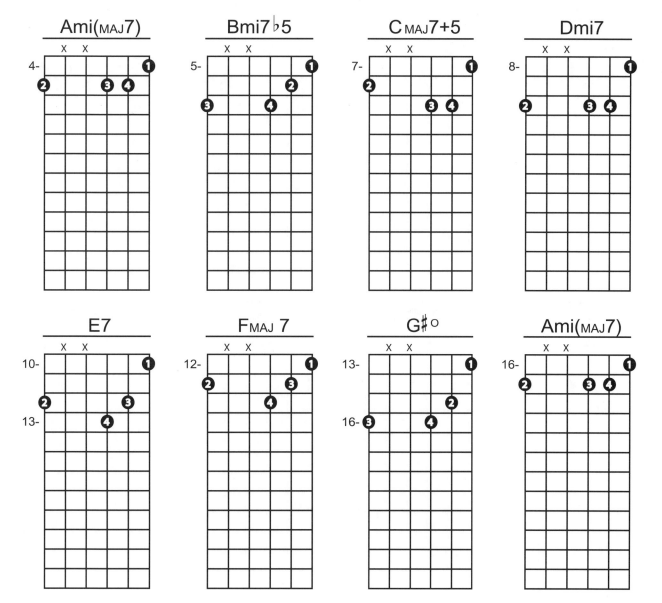

Harmonic Minor 7
Voicing - Root 5, 7, ♭3
Key - C Minor

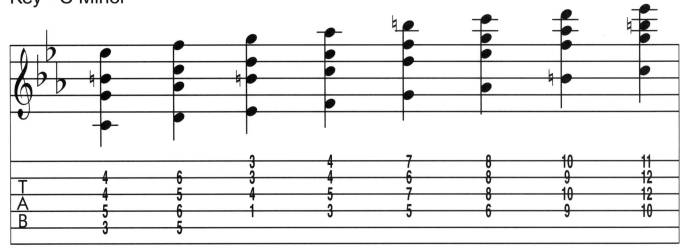

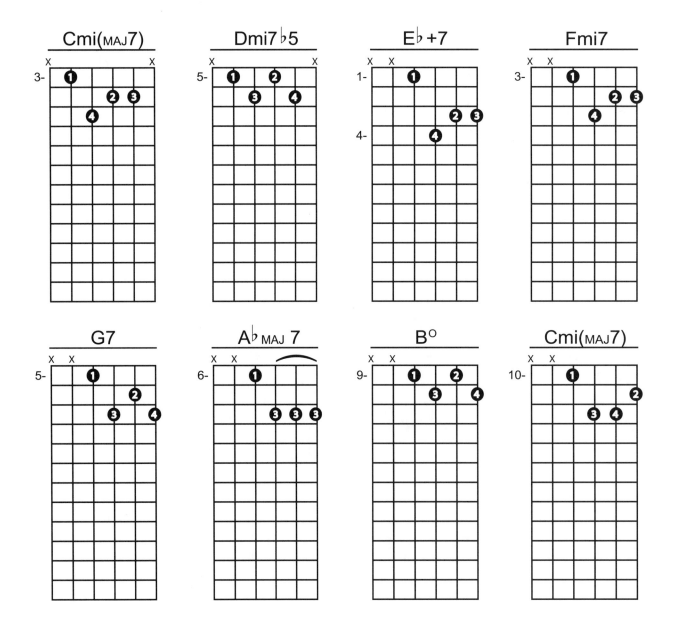

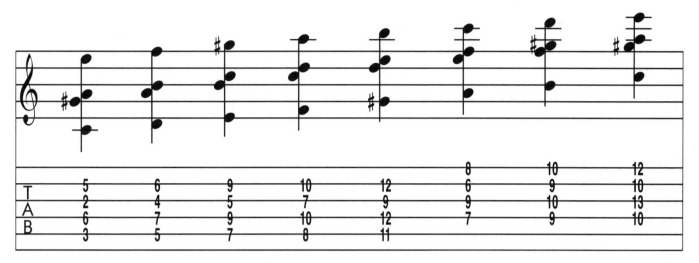

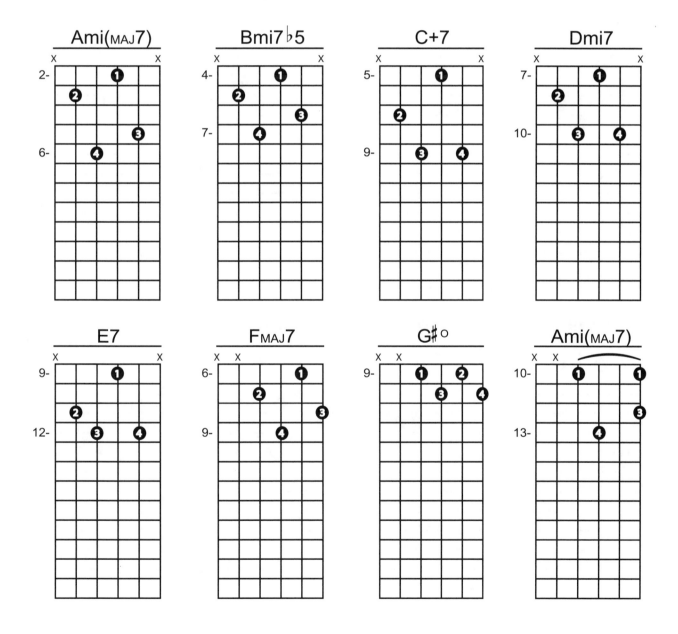

Harmonic Minor 9

* Voicing - Root, ♭3, 7, 9
  Key - D Minor

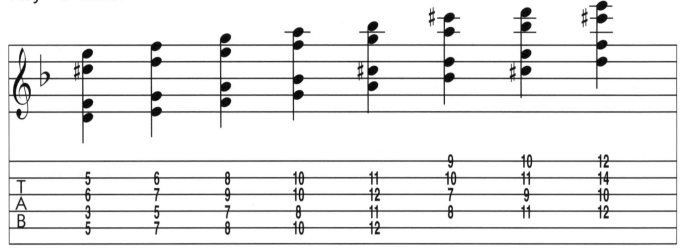

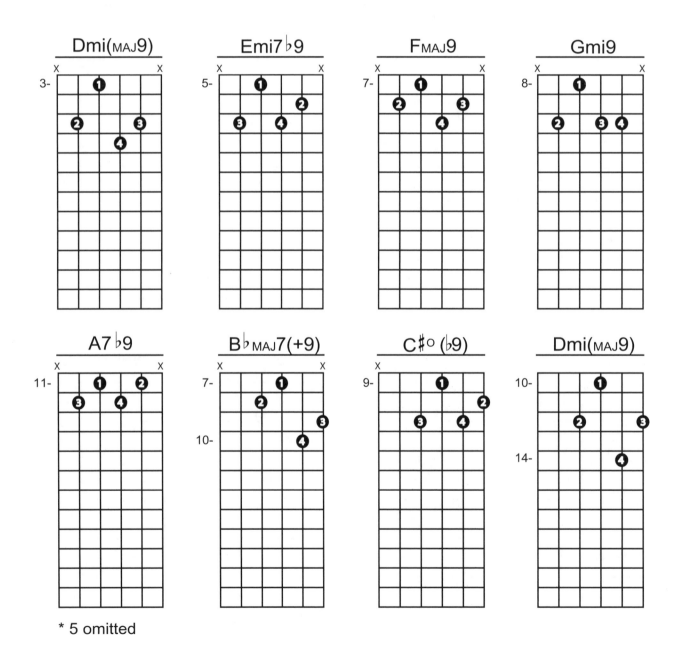

| Dmi(MAJ9) | Emi7♭9 | FMAJ9 | Gmi9 |

| A7♭9 | B♭MAJ7(+9) | C♯o(♭9) | Dmi(MAJ9) |

* 5 omitted

Melodic Minor Triad
Voicing - Root, 5, ♭3
Key - D Minor

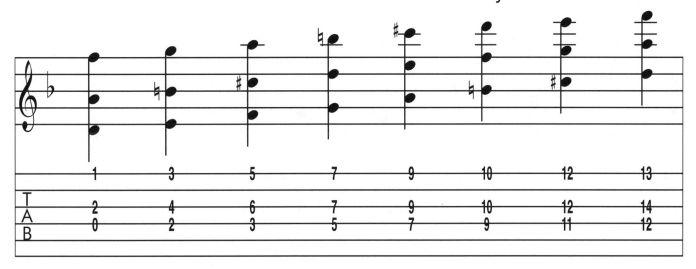

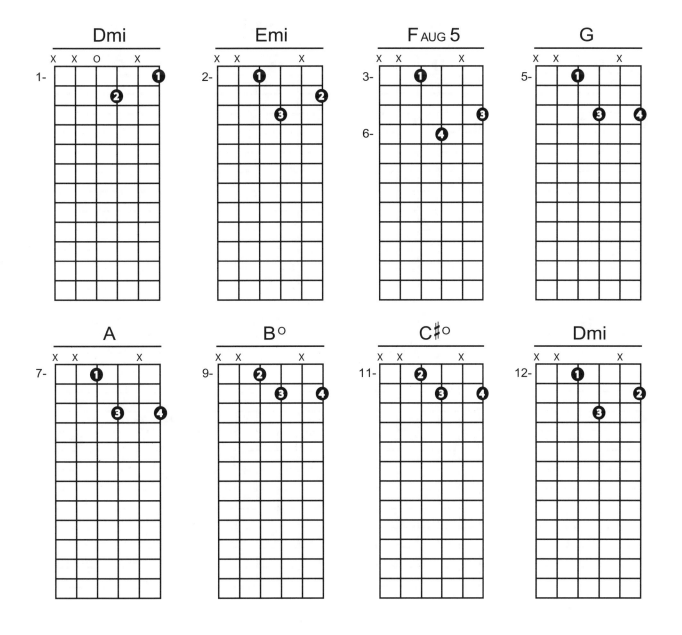

Melodic Minor Triad
Voicing - Root, 5, ♭3
Key - A Minor

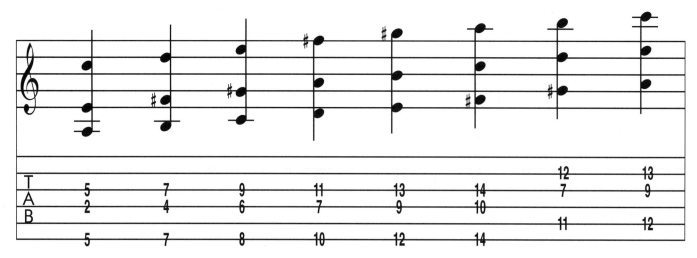

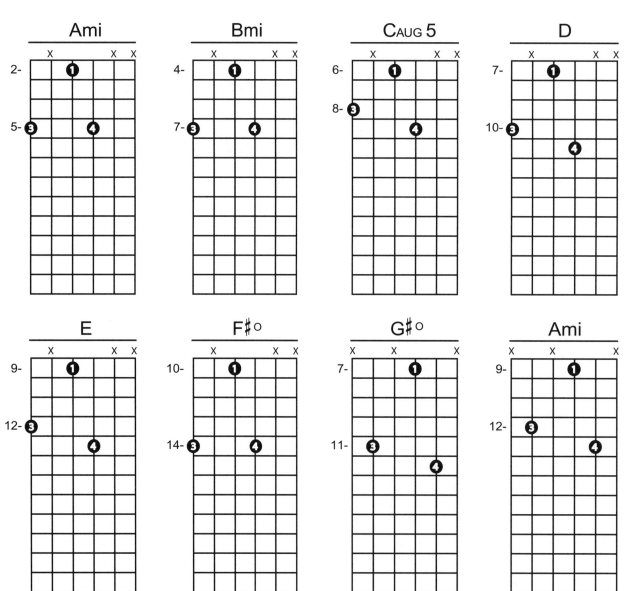

Melodic Minor 6

Voicing - 6, ♭3, 5, Root
Key - A Minor

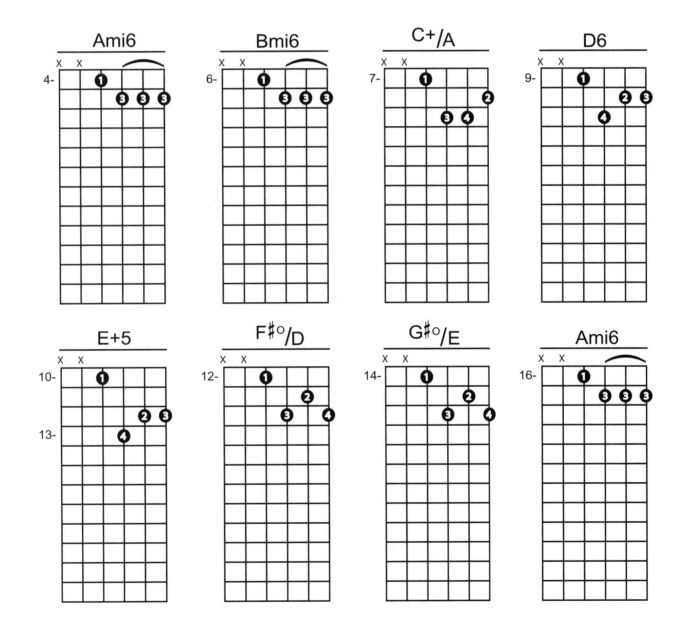

Melodic Minor 7

Voicing - Root, ♭3, 5, 7

Key - A Minor

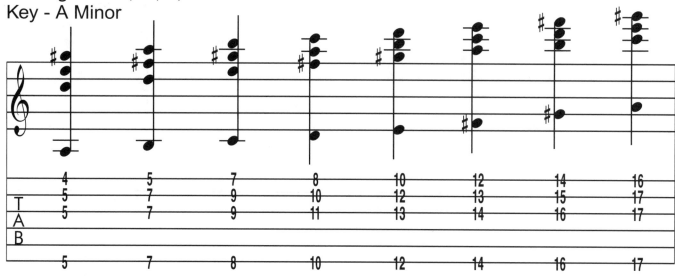

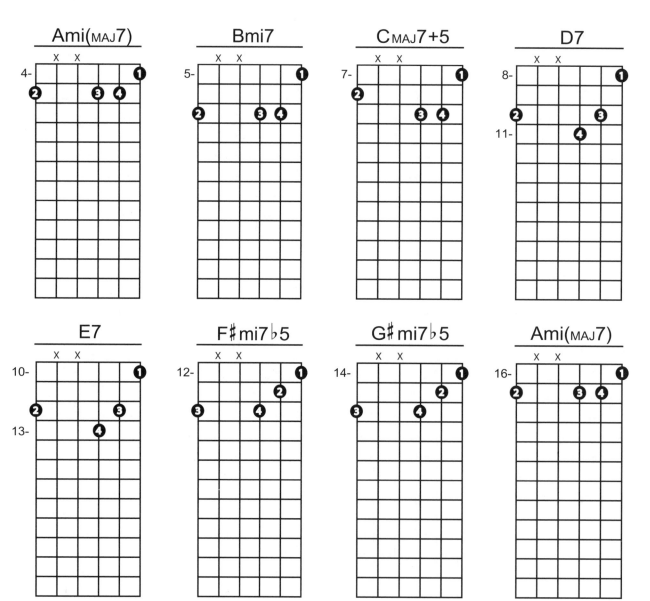

Melodic Minor 9

Voicing - Root, ♭3, 7, 9
Key - D Minor

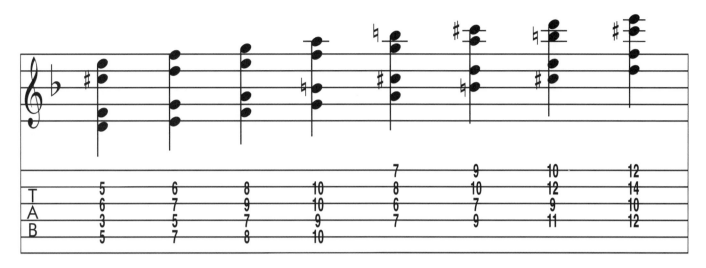

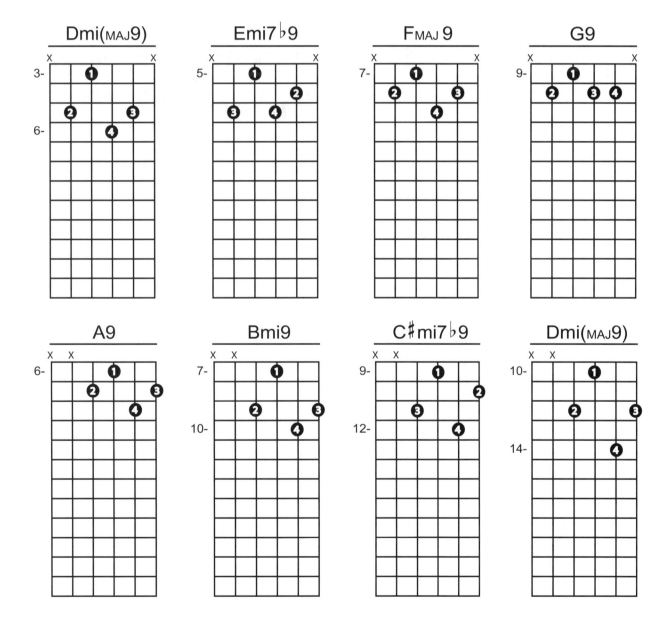

Dominant Chord Scales

| Dominant Triads |
| Dominant 7 |
| Dominant 9 |
| Dominant 13 |

Dominant 7 Triad
Voicing - *Root, 3, ♭7
Key - C

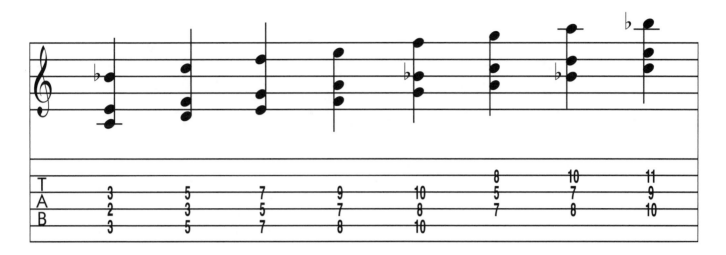

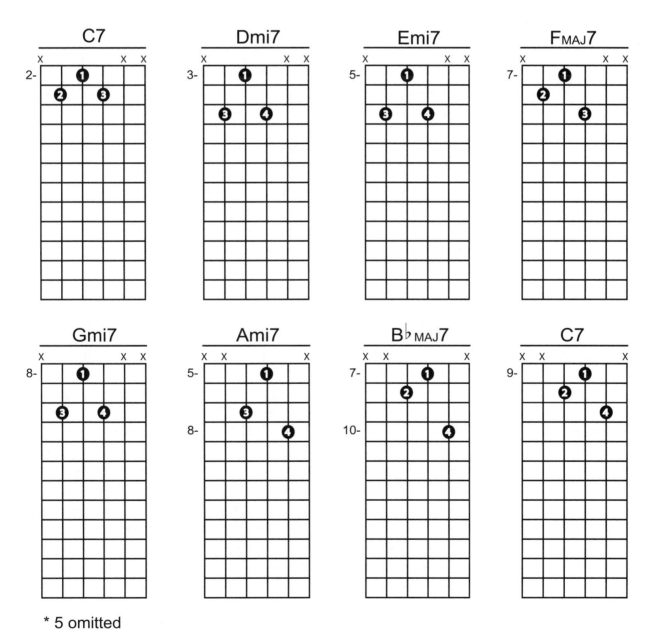

* 5 omitted

Dominant 7 Triad
Voicing - *Root, ♭7, 3
Key - F

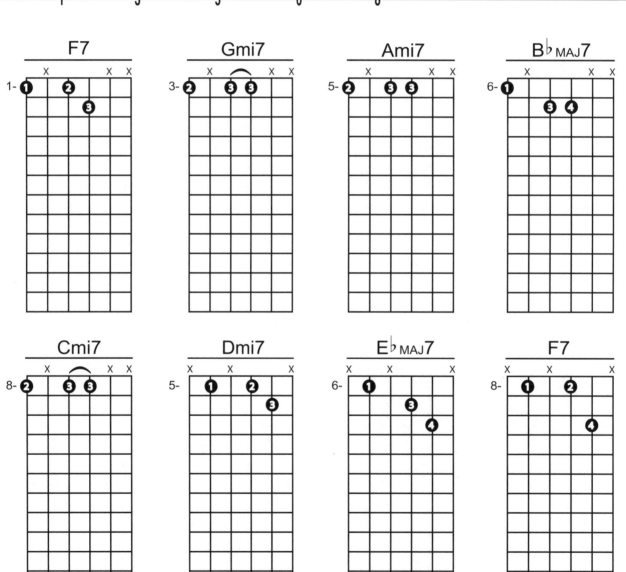

* 5 omitted

Dominant 7 Triad
* Voicing - 3, ♭7, Root
Key - C

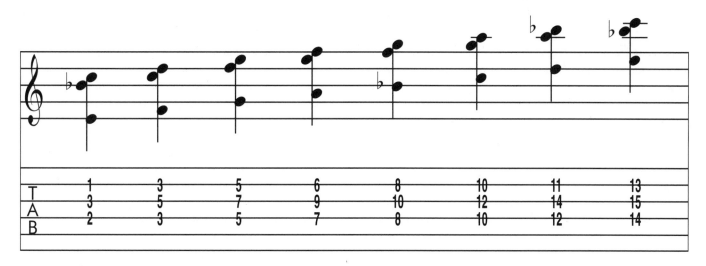

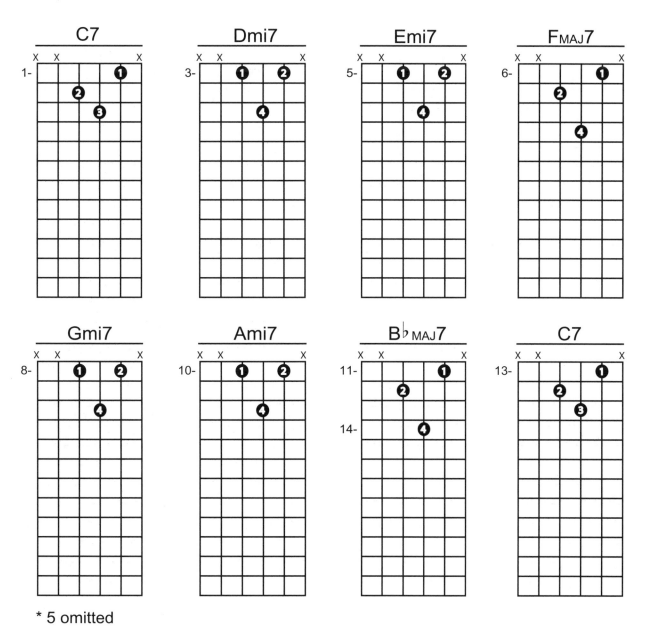

* 5 omitted

Dominant 7 Triad
Voicing - ♭7, Root, 3
Key - C

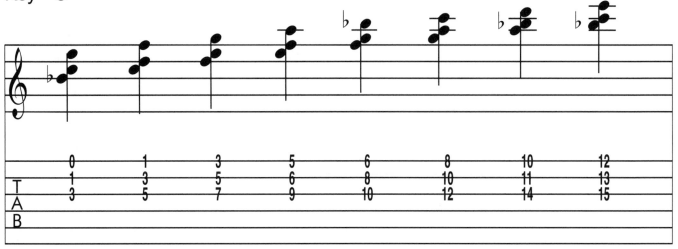

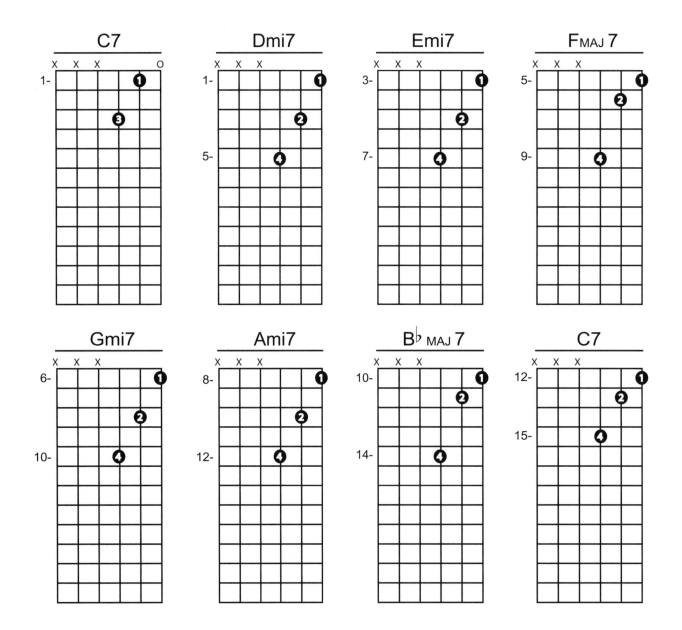

Dominant 7

Voicing - Root, 5, ♭7, 3
Key - C

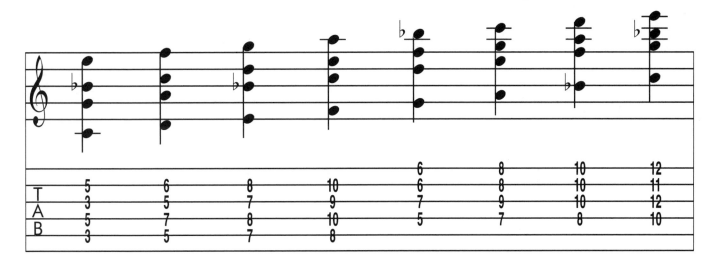

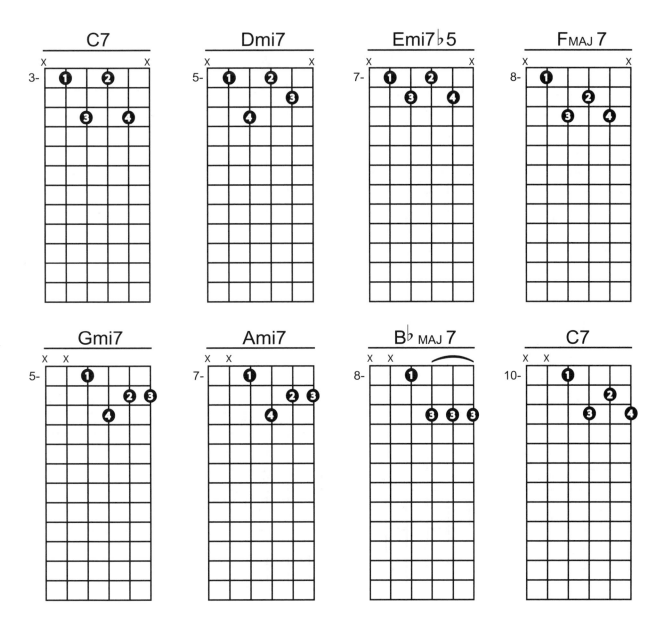

Dominant 7
Voicing - 3, ♭7, Root, 5
Key - C

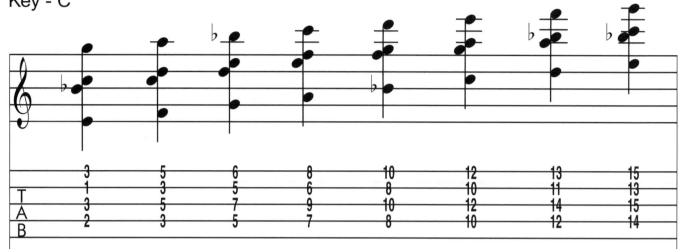

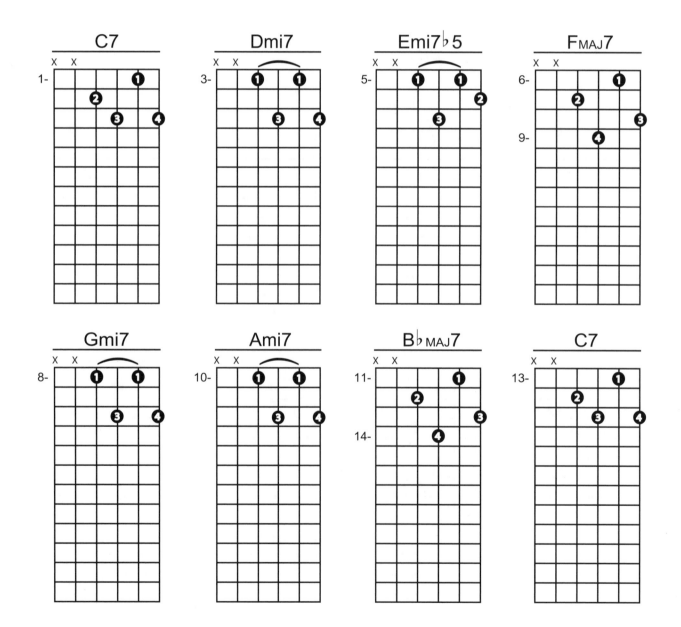

Dominant 7
Voicing - 5, ♭7, Root, 3
Key - C

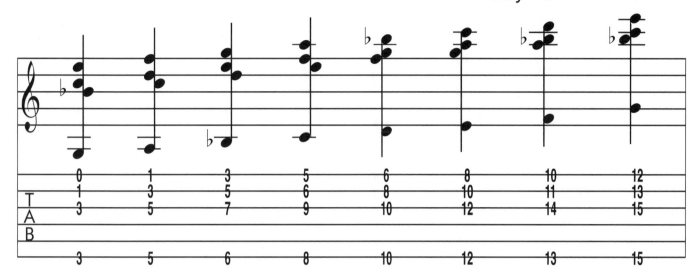

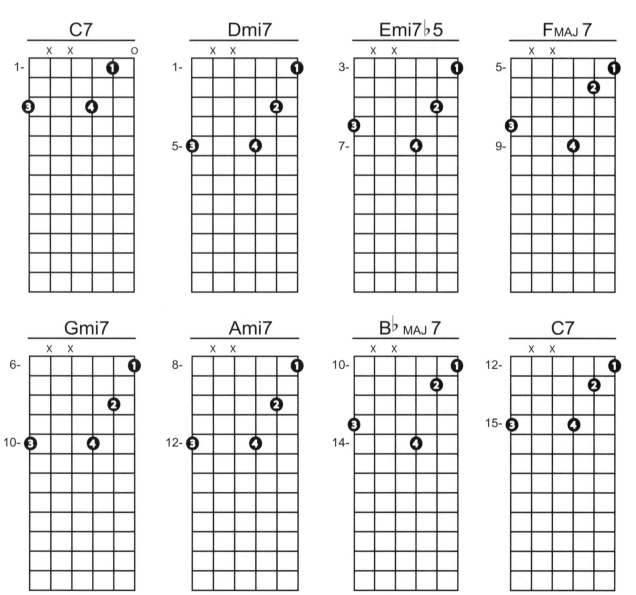

Dominant 7
Voicing - 5, 3, ♭7, Root
Key - C

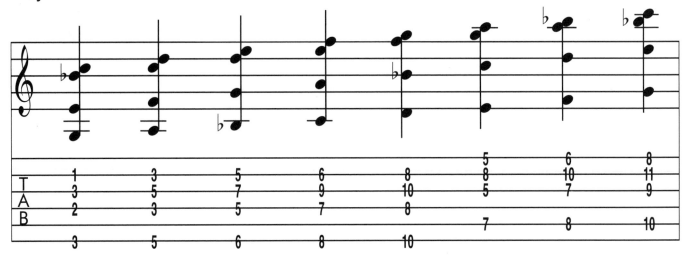

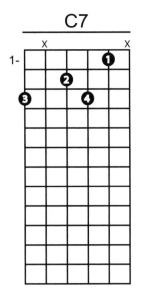

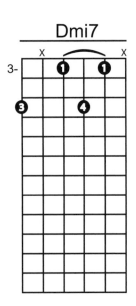

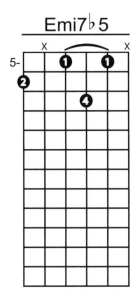

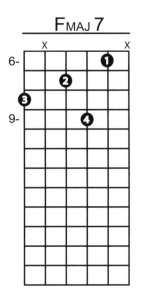

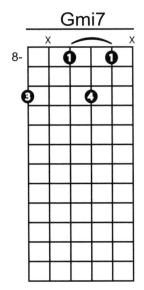

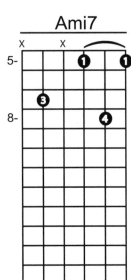

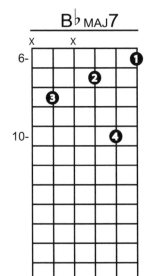

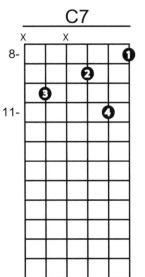

Dominant 9

Voicing - Root, 3, ♭7, 9
Key - C

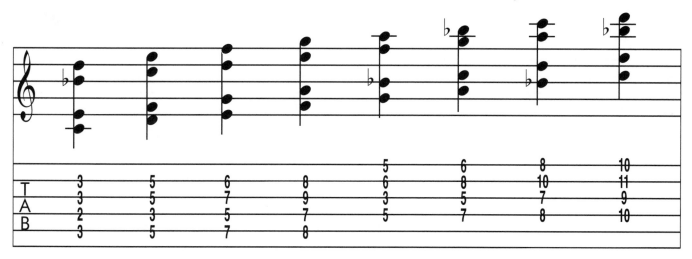

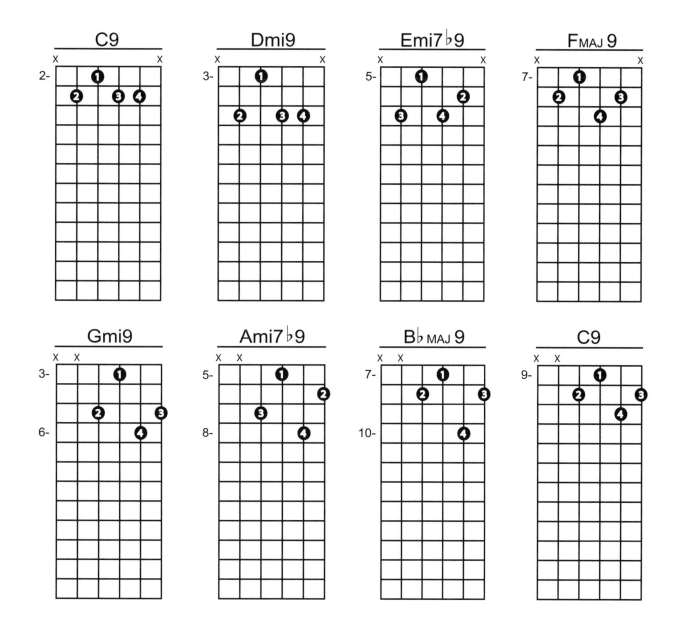

Dominant 9

* Voicing - 5, 9, 3, ♭7
Key - A

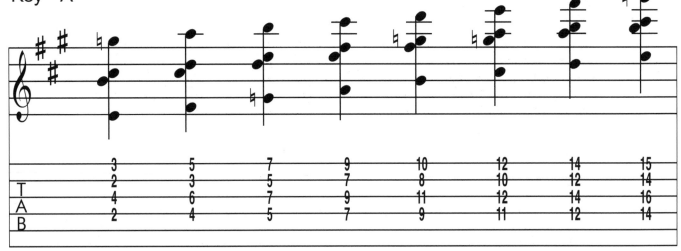

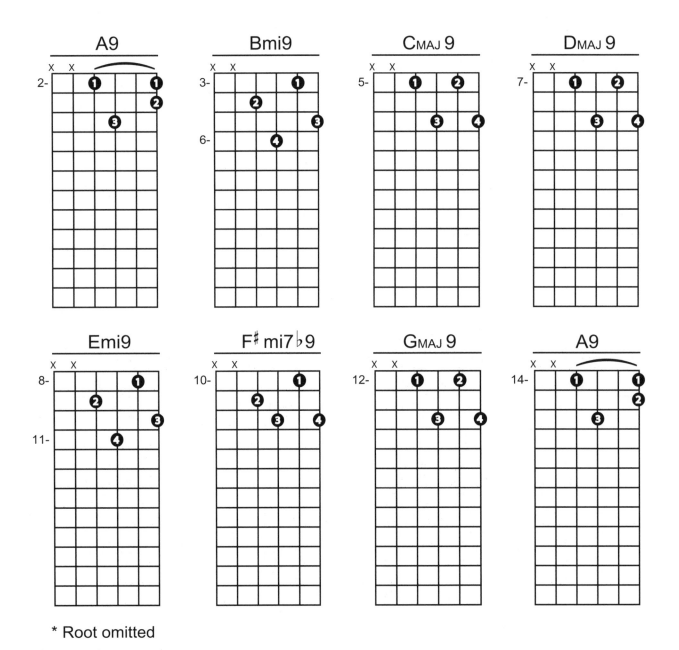

* Root omitted

Dominant 9

* Voicing - ♭7, 3, 5, 9
Key - C

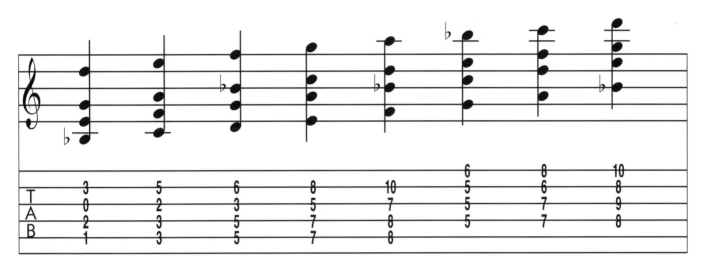

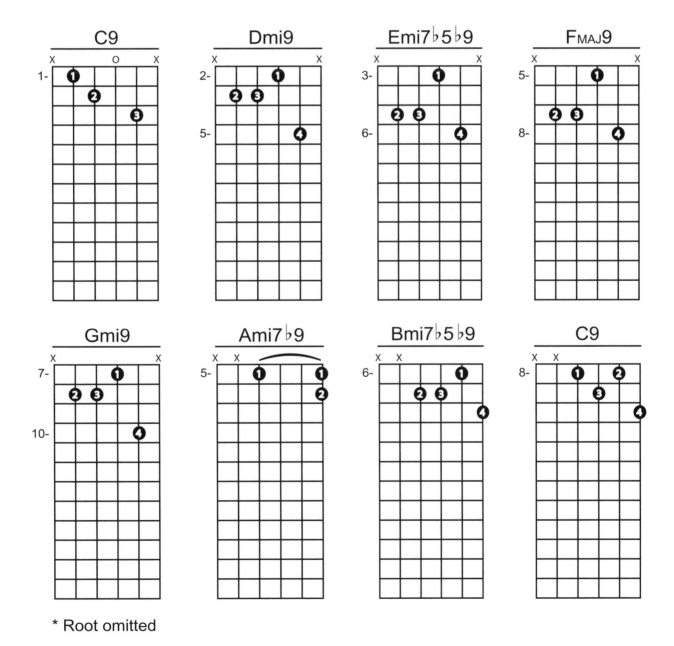

* Root omitted

65

Dominant 9
Voicing - ♭7, 9, 3, Root
Key - G

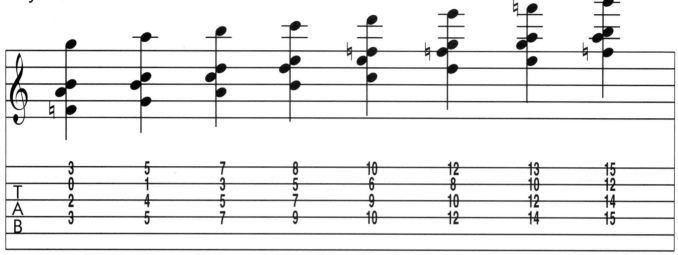

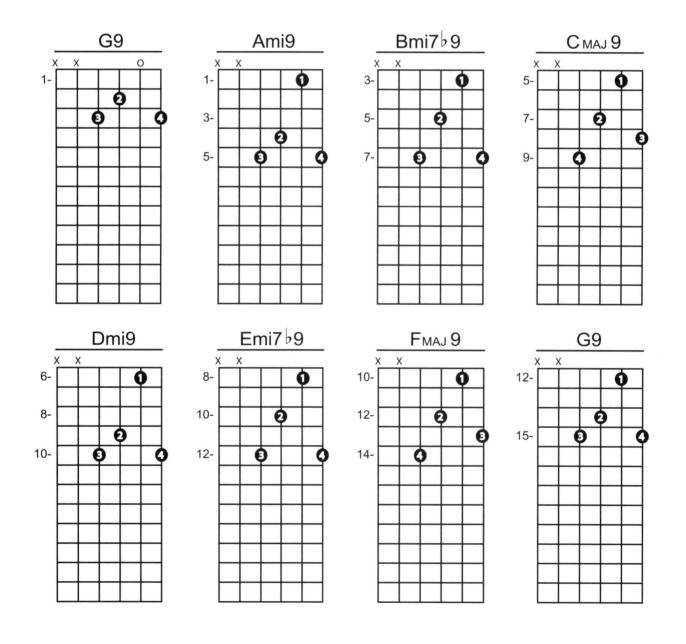

Dominant 13
Voicing - Root, ♭7, 3, 13
Key - C

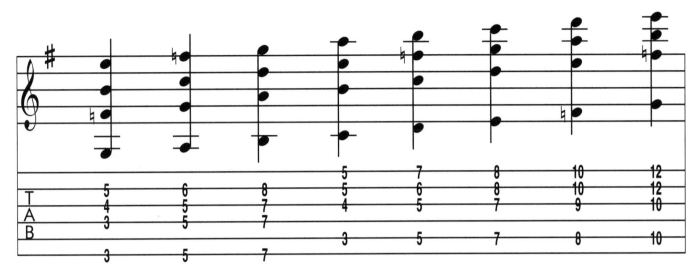

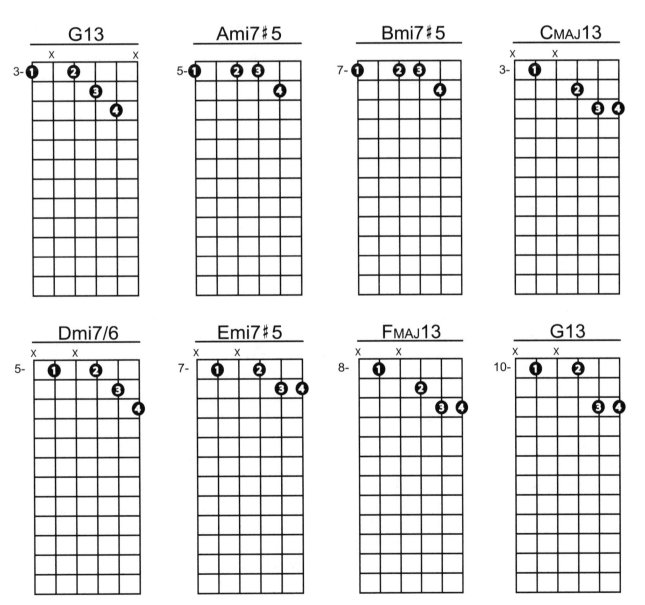

Dominant 13

Voicing - ♭7, 3, 13, 9

Key - C

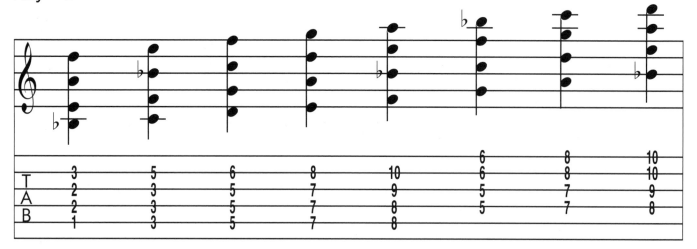

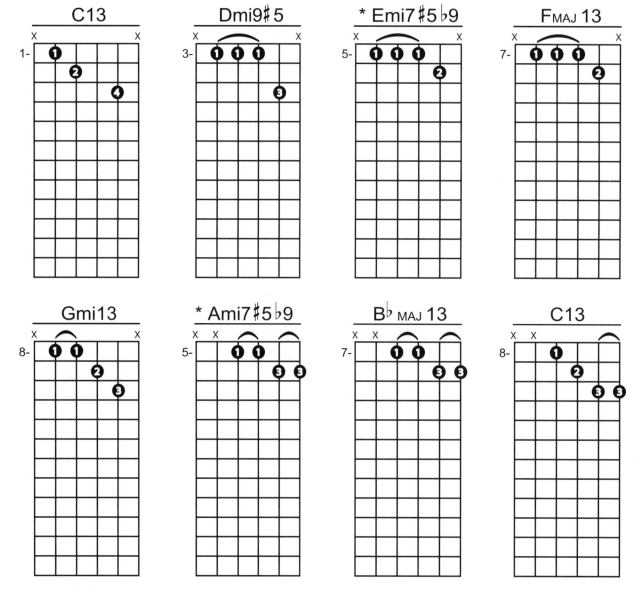

* E-7♯5♭9 = D-11 and E♭MAJ13

* A-7♯5♭9 = A♭MAJ13

About the author

Author	"Melodic Lines for the Intermediate Guitarist" Centerstream Publications/Hal Leonard
Instructor	National Guitar Workshop 2003 - San Francisco, CA National Guitar Workshop 2002 - Los Angeles, CA Private Instruction - Portland, OR~Los Angeles, CA 1979 - 1990 Currently teaches privately in San Francisco, CA
Seminars	Vacuum Tube Valley Magazine - 6550/KT88 Shootout Vacuum Tube Valley Magazine - Ultimate 12AX7 Shootout Vacuum Tube Valley Magazine - Ultimate 6L6 Shootout C.R.I. - San Francisco, CA 1996 Soundmaster Recording - Burbank, CA - 1985 Gold Star Recording Studio - Hollywood ,CA - 1977
Press	Vintage Guitar Magazine - Oct. 2003 - CD "Down to the Wire" Review Guitar One Magazine - Oct. 2003 - Cool New Products - "Melodic Lines..." Vacuum Tube Valley Magazine - 6550/KT88 Shootout - Issue #19 Los Angeles Times - Living Section - April 9, 2002 Vacuum Tube Valley Magazine - Ultimate 12AX7 Shootout - Issue #14 Vacuum Tube Valley Magazine - Ultimate 6L6 Shootout - Issue #13 Guitar Player Magazine - Sessions - Aug. 1999 Guitar Player Magazine - Lick of the Month - Nov. 1998 Guitar for the Practicing Musician - Resume - Sept. 1994 Guitar Player Magazine - Auditions on Call - Apr. 1994
Studied under	Doug MacDonald Phil Upchurch Jimmy Wyble Charlie Shoemake Ron Anthony Jerry Hahn Ted Greene
Album Credits	Greg Cooper - Down to the Wire - 2003 Odyssey - I've got the Melody - RCA - 1982 Michael Wycoff - Come to my World - RCA - 1981 Merry Clayton - Emotion - RCA - 1980 Bill Medley - Unreleased - RCA - 1979
Memberships Endorsements	ASCAP member since 1990 Endorses Heritage Guitars, Kalamazoo, MI
Website	**www.gregcooper-guitar.com**

Also from Greg Cooper

Melodic Lines for the Intermediate Guitarist

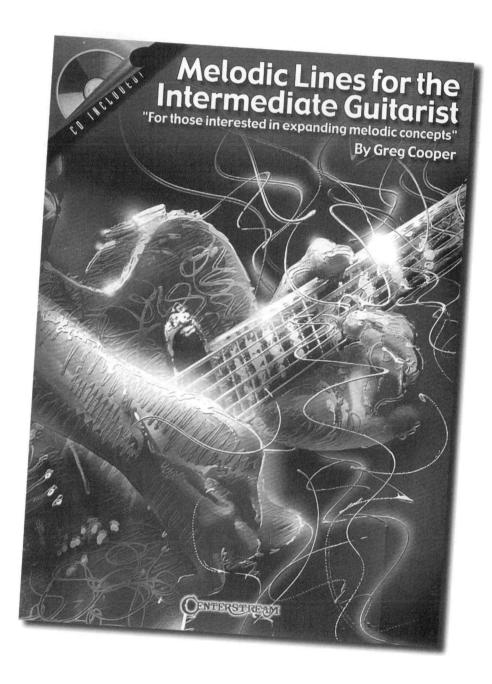

This book/CD pack is essential for anyone interested in expanding their melodic concepts on the guitar. Divided in eight specific chapters author Greg Cooper covers: 1. Picking Exercises, that you can use to warm up, 2. Major Lines played exclusively in a major key or a minor third below, 3. Minor Lines, played exclusively in a minor key or a minor third above, 4. Minor Pentatonic, 5. Dominant Lines, also can be used in the blues context as well as jazz, 6. Altered Lines, generally used in jazz, 7, Blues Turn-arounds, lines to play over the V and IV chords, 8. Jazz Turn-arounds, commonly known as ii-V-I changes. Notated in standard notation and tablature.

00000312 Book/CD pack $19.95